AF322578

A PRACTICAL GUIDE

FAMILY CEO

SHRIHARSH SONAR

HOW TO SECURE YOUR FAMILY'S FUTURE, MANAGE FINANCES, AND PLAN FOR THE UNEXPECTED

Visit www.familyceo.in for more resources and digital tools

Made with ❤ on the Notion Press Platform
www.notionpress.com

Disclaimer

The content, trackers, and suggestions provided in this book and on the **FamilyCEO.in** website are offered for informational purposes only and reflect the views and opinions of the author. This material is not intended to serve as an exhaustive or comprehensive guide to estate planning, financial management, or legal compliance. The user acknowledges that there may be additional steps, measures, and legal considerations required to ensure the protection of one's family and assets, which are not covered in this material.

The information provided, including but not limited to formats for wills, legal documents, and procedures, is of a general nature and is designed to accommodate a global audience. Legal processes, forms, and requirements may vary significantly based on jurisdiction, region, and country. Users are advised that local laws and regulations may impose specific requirements, and it is their responsibility to seek independent legal counsel from a licensed attorney in their respective jurisdiction to ensure that all documents and actions are compliant with applicable laws.

Neither the author nor **FamilyCEO.in** assumes any responsibility or liability for any actions taken based on the suggestions or guidance provided in this book or on the website. The information contained herein does not constitute legal advice, and reliance on the content for legal matters is at the user's own risk. It is strongly recommended that users consult with qualified legal professionals to ensure the validity, enforceability, and compliance of any legal documents or procedures referenced in this book or on the website.

By using this book and the **FamilyCEO.in** website, the user agrees that the author and the platform are not liable for any damages, losses, or legal consequences that may result from following the recommendations, suggestions, or information provided. The content is intended solely for educational and informational purposes and should be used with due diligence and professional consultation.

Dedication

Dearest **Madhura, my beloved wife,** your quiet strength and unwavering courage in the face of an unthinkable challenge have been my constant source of inspiration. As we continue this journey together, facing an illness that no one should have to fight, I have come to understand the depth of our shared fears as parents. The worry about what might happen to our children if we're not here to guide them has weighed heavily on us both.

It is this fear—one that I know every parent in the world shares—that led me to write this book. It's not just a guide; it's a reflection of the love and responsibility we feel for our children's future, and for every family who wonders if they've done enough to protect their loved ones. *Planning for life after life is about ensuring that even in the hardest times, those we cherish most are cared for, with love and security.*

Through it all, your grace and resilience have shaped every word of this book. I dedicate it to you, Madhura, with all my heart and gratitude.

I also want to dedicate the book to the legendary, **Shri Ratan Tata**, whose passing was a profound loss felt across the globe. As I penned the final chapters of this book, I received the heartbreaking news of his departure, and I was reminded of his remarkable legacy.

Sir Ratan Tata exemplified what it means to be a true leader, not only in business but in humanity. His commitment to ethical practices and his dedication to uplifting communities inspire us all to strive for greater purpose. His vision and compassion will forever resonate in the hearts of those he touched.

May Family CEO serve as a tribute to his enduring spirit and the values he championed.

Preface

Life is unpredictable, and I've never felt that more deeply than I do now. For years, I lived as if tomorrow was guaranteed—going to work, raising a family, building a future—never really dwelling on the "what ifs." But this past year turned everything upside down. My spouse was diagnosed with a rare cancer, and suddenly, uncertainty moved into our home. The doctors gave us a time frame—something that could be extended by our fortune or shortened by our fate—but who can really know for sure? At the same time, I find myself questioning my own health, wondering if I'll have enough time—not just in the immediate future, but ten, fifteen, or twenty years down the road—to make sure my family is truly safe and secure.

We are blessed in many ways. We've worked hard and saved enough to take care of our two children, ensuring that they will have a solid financial foundation. But money alone isn't enough. Wealth cannot make decisions for them in our absence. Who will guide them when we're no longer here? How can we ensure that every detail of their lives—education, health, financial well-being—is meticulously planned out, so they are protected even when we're gone?

This is what led me to the idea of creating a website and app—one that can act as a central hub for all the critical information families need during difficult times. Think of it like a personal Facebook for families, not to connect socially but to provide structure, planning, and peace of mind. Wills, financial documents, healthcare instructions—everything parents need to ensure that their children will be taken care of if the worst should happen.

But even this app, as helpful as I hope it will be, isn't enough. I feel there's something more I can offer—a guide, a book. Something simple and concise, no more than one-fifty pages, that can walk parents through the steps they need to take to become what I call the **Family**

CEO. This book is a reflection of my own journey—a guide for parents like me, who want to take control of their family's future but feel overwhelmed by the weight of it all.

I've kept this book short on purpose. I want it to be something you can read in one sitting, and something that every parent, regardless of where they live, can adapt to their own family's needs. At the end of each chapter, I've added trackers that you can fill in manually with a black ink pen, allowing you to document important information in one place. Once completed, you can keep the book in a safe custody or locker, so that in the unfortunate event that your children or either parent haven't opened the account on the website, they can simply read the book and act accordingly. My hope is that this idea—this concept of being the CEO of your family—will resonate not just with people who are facing their own health challenges, but with every parent who wants to leave behind more than just memories.

I invite you to take this journey with me, to step into the role of the Family CEO, and create a lasting impact on the lives of your children, even when you're no longer here to guide them. After all, ensuring their future is the greatest legacy any of us can leave behind.

~FCA Shriharsh Sonar

P.S. Remember, when your time comes, you won't get even a second extra. Cherish every moment and prepare wisely—*you may not have the chance to say goodbye.*

Building the Future on Our Past:
The Power of Family Trees (Vanshaval)

The concept of Vanshaval refers to a family lineage or genealogy record, typically documenting the ancestry of a family across generations. In many Indian traditions, especially in Hindu culture, Vanshaval or ***Vanshavali is a detailed family tree*** that records names, relationships, and important events associated with ancestors. This information is often preserved and passed down through generations, serving as a historical record of a family's heritage and identity. It allows us to understand our lineage, celebrate our heritage, and ensure that the contributions and stories of our ancestors are never lost to time.

Traditionally, Vanshaval is used to trace one's roots and understand the connections that link families over time. It gives a sense of belonging and continuity, helping future generations understand their place within a broader historical context. In some families, these records are maintained as official documents, often written on paper or preserved in traditional formats like scrolls, with each generation contributing to its upkeep. However, in the digital age, this valuable tradition risks being lost, as fewer people take the time to document family history in detail.

To honor and continue this tradition, I have created a ***Family Tree tracker*** in a separate chapter of this book. This tracker will help you document your lineage and add your own stories, ensuring that this important information is not only preserved but also easily accessible for future generations. By maintaining and updating this family history, we can make sure that our roots are remembered, our stories are celebrated, and, from now on, in the digital world, this record will be maintained perpetually. I urge all parents and upcoming generations to contribute to this record so that our heritage continues to be honored, appreciated, and passed down for years to come.

Introduction

Why Every Parent is a Family CEO

We often hear the term "CEO" and immediately think of corporate boardrooms, large offices, and executive decision-making. But what if I told you that, as a parent, you are already the CEO of your most valuable enterprise—your family?

The role of a parent goes beyond simply nurturing and providing for your children. You manage finances, make long-term plans, navigate crises, and ensure that every aspect of your family's well-being is taken care of. While CEOs oversee the success of a company, parents oversee something much more precious: the happiness, security, and future of their loved ones. This is why I believe every parent is a Family CEO.

The Unseen Role We Play

As parents, we carry enormous responsibilities. We juggle day-to-day tasks—planning meals, managing school schedules, coordinating doctor visits, paying bills, and planning for future milestones like college or weddings. But beyond the surface, we are also the architects of our family's future. We make decisions that impact not just the present but the years and generations to come.

Financial decisions are central to this role, whether we realize it or not. From budgeting and saving to investing in education and planning for retirement, we are constantly making choices that will shape our children's future. And it's not just about money. We are also the keepers of health records, legal documents, and crucial information that our family will need when we're no longer around.

Why the Family CEO Concept Matters

When we think about the role of a CEO, we imagine someone who makes strategic decisions to ensure the growth and success of a company. They don't leave things to chance—they plan, they delegate, they take control. Similarly, parents are the ones who make sure that, in both good times and bad, their families are safe and secure.

However, many of us leave gaps in this plan, especially when it comes to preparing for the unexpected. Have we arranged our affairs in such a way that, if we were no longer here tomorrow, our children and loved ones could navigate the complexities of life without added stress? Could they access bank accounts, settle debts, or even find important documents like a will or insurance policies?

The truth is, most of us don't have a complete plan in place. As parents, we get so caught up in the busyness of daily life that we sometimes overlook these critical tasks. But as CEOs of our family, it's our duty to make sure that all of these elements are neatly organized and accessible, even if we're not there to manage them ourselves.

The Common Concerns Every Parent Faces

When you bring a child into the world, your mind is flooded with worries and concerns. You think about their education, their health, their happiness. You want to give them the best start in life, and you work hard to make sure they have everything they need. But as they grow older, new questions start to arise: ***What if I'm not around to help them when they need it most?***

This fear of the unknown is one of the most common concerns for parents. We often ask ourselves:

- Who will take care of my children if something happens to me?

- Will they have the resources they need to continue their education or pursue their dreams?

- How will they navigate the complexities of life—managing finances, handling legal matters, or dealing with unexpected crises—without my guidance?

These concerns keep many parents awake at night, and rightfully so. It's not just about the material things we leave behind; it's about the knowledge, structure, and security we provide that will enable our children to thrive in our absence.

My Own Journey: A Personal Reflection

I never fully realized the weight of these responsibilities until recently. My spouse's diagnosis with a rare form of cancer and the doubts surrounding my own long-term health made everything come into sharp focus. Suddenly, the "what ifs" that I had pushed to the back of my mind became urgent, pressing questions.

We've been fortunate in many ways—financially stable, with the resources to care for our children. But one question loomed large in my mind: ***Have I done enough to prepare them for a future without us?*** I realized that I hadn't fully organized the details of our family's financial and legal matters. Important documents were scattered, passwords were saved in different places, and our children wouldn't have the first clue about where to start if something happened to us.

It was this personal wake-up call that led me to the idea of creating a website, an app, and now this book. I wanted to create a simple, practical guide that parents like me could follow to ensure their families would be taken care of, no matter what. I realized that just like a CEO, I had to organize, manage, and protect the "company" that is my family.

My Father-in-Law's Story: The Hidden Complexity of Disciplines

My father-in-law was a remarkably disciplined man. He was organized to the point that he kept meticulous records of everything—his finances, investments, and personal documents. From the outside, it seemed that if anything were to happen to him, the family would have no difficulty handling his affairs.

Unfortunately, reality had other plans. He passed away suddenly one evening due to a blood clot that blocked the vein supplying oxygen to his brain. No one was prepared for this, especially since he had never shared the full details of his financial situation or health condition. He had known for a while that he had a blockage in his heart, but he hadn't mentioned it to us. It was as if he believed that by keeping quiet, he could somehow manage everything on his own, sparing the family the worry.

After his passing, when we went through his personal files, we were overwhelmed by the complexity of what he had left behind. There were mutual funds, numerous post office schemes (which were popular forms of saving back then), multiple bank accounts, and several ongoing communications from these institutions. Statements arrived on a quarterly, half-yearly, or yearly basis, but he had never sat down to consolidate or share this information with anyone.

To make things even more complicated, he had changed his will several times. Some drafts were half-complete, and others were finalized. He had altered the distribution of his assets between his wife, daughter, and son. For example, his jewelry was divided between his wife, daughter, and daughter-in-law, stored in two different lockers. His three house properties were allocated in varying proportions between his children, and the nominations on these properties were updated from time to time.

It took months, if not years, of effort to untangle this web and clearly understand his final wishes. The entire process was emotionally exhausting and time-consuming, a burden on the very people he was trying to protect. His desire to control everything without sharing his plans created unnecessary stress and confusion for the family.

This experience opened my eyes to the importance of clear communication, transparency, and thorough planning. As much as we want to manage things on our own, failing to involve our loved ones can create more chaos than we ever intend.

The Businessman's Family: The Complexities After Sudden Loss

In the old days, when we were living in a large housing colony, most families—about 50 in total—knew each other well. We were on the 6th floor, and just two floors below us, on the 4th, lived a gentle, polite, and generous businessman. He was a kind soul, always willing to help, and it wasn't until much later that I came to fully understand how successful and respected he was.

During one of the Ganesha festivals, our society decided to build a temple in the colony to honor Lord Ganesha. To everyone's surprise and delight, this man offered the largest contribution. Not only did he cover the cost of construction, but he also donated the idol itself. It was an incredible gesture, and it showed the kind of person he was—always ready to give.

Unfortunately, just two days after making that generous offer, tragedy struck. It was 1:00 a.m. when we received a call from the police station in a nearby town, about 30 kilometers away. His truck had been involved in an accident while returning from a ghat section, and four lives were lost in the crash, including his. As members of the same society, we took on the painful responsibility of bringing the bodies back and organizing the cremation.

The real tragedy, though, was that he left behind a wife and three small daughters. His wife had no idea about his business affairs, which were managed by three partners. In the beginning, even his partners expressed grief, but soon their attitudes began to change. After a few weeks, we started to sense something was amiss. The business partners, who had shared in his success, were now avoiding the topic of compensating his family, refusing to pay them the share that rightfully belonged to his wife and children.

Being a chartered accountant, I stepped in to help, leveraging my experience and the support of some powerful friends in our building. It was a difficult, months-long process, poring over his financials and negotiating on behalf of his wife. The partners were evasive and resistant, but after six months of tough discussions, we were able to secure a fair settlement for her.

In addition to this, we had to deal with outstanding home loan liabilities and negotiate with the insurance company and the transport company involved in the accident to ensure his family received all the compensation they deserved. His wife was eventually left with enough resources to manage their family's finances, cover educational costs for the children, and pay off the home loan.

This experience showed me, once again, how fragile life can be and how quickly things can unravel in the absence of clear financial plans. Despite his good nature and success, the businessman's sudden death left his family in turmoil—emotionally, financially, and legally. If he had just taken the time to share his business details with his wife or properly documented his plans, the aftermath would have been far less stressful for those left behind. It's these real-world experiences that have solidified my belief in the need for a tool like the Family CEO app, and why I've decided to write this book.

Imagine this: You're on a family vacation. You're sitting on the beach, watching your children play in the waves. You feel a sense of peace wash over you, knowing that your family is happy and safe. But somewhere in the back of your mind, a little voice whispers: *What would happen if I wasn't here?*

Suddenly, the picture changes. You're no longer on vacation. You're in the hospital, dealing with an emergency, and you realize that there's so much left unfinished. Your family doesn't know the passwords to your accounts, they don't know where you keep your will, and they have no idea how to handle the financial details that will inevitably come up.

This is not a scenario we like to think about, but it's one that could happen to any of us. And while we can't predict the future, we can prepare for it. *That's what it means to be the Family CEO—taking control of the unknown so that, even in our absence, our families can continue to thrive.*

In the following chapters, I'll guide you through the steps of becoming your family's CEO. We'll cover everything from creating a family tree for future generations, to organizing financial documents, to planning for your children's education, and even handling the more sensitive matters like funeral arrangements and last wishes. By the end of this journey, you'll have a clear plan in place, ensuring that your family will be taken care of, no matter what life throws your way.

Because, at the end of the day, the greatest gift you can give your family is the security of knowing.

They'll be okay—even when you're not there to guide them!

Tracking Your Information: In the Book or Online

Whether you choose to maintain the information manually in this book or digitally on the website, **The Family CEO** platform is designed to provide peace of mind to families by organizing and safeguarding critical information. The following trackers serve as essential tools for documenting and managing all aspects of a family's financial, legal, and personal matters, ensuring that important data is accessible when needed most. These trackers are easily available on **www.familyceo.in**, but if you prefer to maintain them on your own, here is a comprehensive list to guide you in keeping your information organized and accessible.

1. **Financial Portfolio Tracker**

   Keeping track of all financial assets (bank accounts, investments, loans) in one place helps ensure that in case of emergencies, your family can easily access and manage financial resources without unnecessary delays or confusion.

2. **Real Estate Tracker**

   Managing real estate properties, mortgages, and rental agreements is often complex. This tracker simplifies the process by clearly documenting property ownership, mortgage details, and rental agreements, preventing any mismanagement or loss of property information.

3. **Inventory of Valuables Tracker**

   High-value items such as jewelry, art, or collectibles often become difficult to manage after the passing of the family head. This tracker ensures that all valuables are documented, appraised, and stored securely for future reference.

4. **Warranties & Guarantees Tracker**
   Expensive assets are usually covered by warranties or guarantees. Tracking this information ensures that repairs or replacements can be requested when necessary, saving the family both time and money.

5. **Liabilities Tracker**
   Understanding and settling outstanding debts like loans and mortgages is crucial after the family head's passing. This tracker helps document all liabilities, ensuring that payments are up to date and allowing for clear financial management.

6. **Children's Education Tracker**
   Education expenses, especially for overseas education or long-term planning, can be complex. This tracker ensures all fees, scholarships, and future educational goals are documented, giving clarity on education costs and financial commitments.

7. **Health & Medical Information Tracker**
   Proper medical documentation can make a world of difference in emergencies. This tracker organizes medical records, ongoing treatments, and health insurance policies, ensuring your family is prepared for any medical situation.

8. **Digital Assets Tracker**
   In today's digital world, online accounts, subscriptions, and digital legacies need to be managed securely. This tracker helps store credentials and manage access to digital assets, protecting your family's online presence.

9. **Wills & Legal Documents Tracker**
   Wills, trusts, and other legal documents are critical for family succession planning. This tracker ensures that these documents are easily accessible, up-to-date, and in line with your wishes, preventing legal disputes.

10. **Employment Benefits Tracker**
    Employer-provided benefits like gratuity, provident fund, and retirement plans are essential sources of financial security. This tracker ensures that

all employment-related benefits are properly documented and accessible to your family.

11. **Charity & Philanthropy Tracker**

Philanthropic contributions are an important part of many families' legacies. This tracker documents planned donations and endowments, ensuring that charitable goals are honored and carried forward.

12. **Funeral Arrangements Tracker**

By documenting funeral preferences, last rites, and organ donation wishes, this tracker helps your family honor your final wishes and avoid the stress of planning during a difficult time.

13. **Pet Care Tracker**

Pets are family too. This tracker documents veterinarian contacts, feeding schedules, and caregivers, ensuring that your pets are taken care of even if you're not around.

14. **Business Ownership & Succession Planning Tracker**

For business owners, succession planning is vital to ensure the business continues running smoothly. This tracker helps document business ownership, financials, and succession plans to guide the transition.

15. **Security & Permissions Tracker**

Managing access to financial and personal information is critical for both security and continuity. This tracker organizes permissions and access control for family members, advisors, and business partners.

16. **Nominations Tracker**

Proper nomination management is essential for financial assets like bank accounts and investments. This tracker ensures that the right nominees are recorded and easily accessible.

17. **Trusts Management Tracker**

For families with minors or dependents, managing trusts can be complex. This tracker documents trust details, assets, and the roles of trustees, simplifying trust management.

18. **Tax & Legal Matters Tracker**

Keeping up with tax filings and legal matters is crucial for financial stability. This tracker helps your family stay on top of pending tax liabilities and legal obligations, preventing penalties or legal issues.

19. **Emergency Contacts Tracker**

Having a clear list of emergency contacts is essential in crisis situations. This tracker provides all the necessary contact information for key advisors, healthcare providers, and family members, ensuring help is only a call away.

20. **Family Tree Tracker**

Understanding your family lineage and preserving your family's legacy is important for future generations. This tracker documents family history, relationships, and key milestones, creating a lasting record.

21. **Document Vault Tracker**

Critical documents need to be securely stored and easily accessible. This tracker provides a centralized vault for personal identification, financial, legal, and other important documents.

22. **Emergency Funds Tracker**

Immediate access to emergency funds can make all the difference for your family during crises. This tracker ensures that emergency reserves, insurance payouts, and short-term investments are easily available.

23. **Managing trusts for Special Needs Care**

To ensure that all critical information related to Special needs children and their care, finances, medical needs, and education is well-organized and easily accessible.

24. **Closing Accounts in Case of Death Tracker**

After a family head's passing, closing accounts efficiently is vital for financial management. This tracker provides step-by-step guidance for closing bank accounts, settling loans, and handling digital assets.

The Role of a Family CEO

As a parent or the head of the family, you're much more than a caregiver or provider. Whether you realize it or not, you're also the Chief Executive Officer (CEO) of your household. This title isn't about holding power or making executive decisions in a corporate boardroom; rather, it's about shouldering responsibilities and ensuring the well-being of your family. In many ways, a family CEO manages the financial health, security, and future of the household, just as a business CEO manages the growth and sustainability of a company.

Taking Charge: The Everyday Role of a Family CEO

The family CEO's role starts with simple, everyday tasks—managing household budgets, ensuring the bills are paid, and keeping track of savings. But it goes far beyond these basics. It extends to planning for the future, navigating unexpected challenges, and securing the legacy you leave behind for your loved ones. Much like a business, a family has both assets and liabilities, and as the head of the family, it's your job to make sure everything is in order.

A family CEO takes charge of the following key areas:

1. **Managing Finances:** As the head of your family, you're responsible for overseeing all financial aspects—keeping track of bank accounts, paying off debts, and managing investments. These might seem like mundane tasks, but they're the foundation of financial security. Being organized with your money now ensures your family is secure later. Financial management also means understanding the risks involved in various investments and how to protect your assets.

2. **Asset Management:** Beyond finances, you manage tangible assets like property, valuables, vehicles, and even digital assets. This might include keeping up with mortgage payments or car loans, maintaining documents for warranties and guarantees on big-ticket items, or ensuring that the family's digital footprint is secure and well-managed.

3. **Key Decision-Making:** Just as a CEO makes decisions that steer the future of a company, a family CEO is responsible for making decisions that will impact the family for generations. This includes everything from deciding on long-term investments to figuring out the best way to secure

your children's education, to setting up wills and succession plans. Each decision impacts not only the current family members but also future generations.

Leadership, Planning, and Legacy

A family CEO is not just a manager but also a leader. *Leadership within a family isn't about commanding or controlling—it's about setting the right course and guiding your loved ones through life's complexities.* This involves strategic thinking, planning for the future, and ensuring that your family is well-prepared to face challenges, even when you're no longer there to guide them.

Much like *a CEO builds a team that can function independently in their absence, a family CEO empowers family members with the knowledge and resources they need.* This might mean teaching children about financial responsibility, ensuring your spouse knows where to find important documents, or having an open conversation about the family's financial health. The idea is to leave behind a roadmap that your family can follow even if you aren't around to guide them.

At the heart of this responsibility is *legacy.* When we talk about legacy, we aren't just referring to financial inheritance, but also to the values, principles, and life lessons you pass on. Much like how a successful company continues to thrive after its founder steps down, your family should have the tools to carry on smoothly, even in your absence. This is where careful planning comes in.

Keeping It Simple: Relating to Everyday Life!

Being a family CEO doesn't mean handling everything like a business professional. It's about simplifying complicated matters so they can be easily understood by your family. Whether it's explaining how a savings account works to your teenage children or organizing important documents in a way that anyone can access, the role of a family CEO is to make life easier for everyone involved.

For example, instead of seeing the management of finances as an intimidating task, think of it as just organizing your pantry. Everything has a place, every jar is labeled, and every ingredient is easy to find when needed.

Similarly, keeping track of your finances, assets, and liabilities should follow the same principle—organized, clear, and accessible.

Another relatable example is planning for your children's future education. Just as you'd research schools, compare fees, and look into extracurricular activities, as the family CEO, you also plan for how you'll fund their education, considering scholarships, savings, or even long-term investments. In doing so, you create a path they can walk without worrying about finances later. Even if they wish to pursue overseas education, your departure should not be a final verdict on their dreams, forcing them to change courses just to accommodate your absence.

An ideal family CEO ensures that everything runs smoothly, even in their absence. While nothing can replace your presence, it shouldn't mean that your family's fate must change forever. ***You should provide for all possible adversities in life—not to predict them, but to prepare.*** If those adversities never come, then you're extraordinarily lucky. But if they do, you will have ensured that luck doesn't interfere with the lives of your loved ones, and they can carry on with the life you envisioned for them.

Building a Strong Foundation

Ultimately, being the head of the family, the "Family CEO," means being proactive. ***You're not waiting for life to happen; you're planning for it, building a secure foundation*** so that your family thrives no matter what challenges come their way. Like any CEO, you balance short-term needs with long-term goals, always with an eye on securing a better future for the ones you love.

In the end, it's about leading with love and responsibility. While being a family CEO involves managing tangible and financial assets, it's also about creating emotional security, establishing trust, and ensuring that your family is prepared for all eventualities.

"*After my father passed away, we spent months piecing together his financial assets from different banks and investments. If we had a tool like Family CEO, with everything documented in one place, it would have saved us from a lot of unnecessary stress during an already difficult time.*"

- Sachin Patankar, Pune

Chapter 1: Taking Stock of Your Family's Financial Situation

"A WELL-ORGANIZED FINANCIAL PORTFOLIO IS A ROADMAP THAT TURNS CHAOS INTO CLARITY FOR YOUR LOVED ONES WHEN THEY NEED IT MOST."

One of the biggest challenges families face after the sudden death of a parent is understanding where the financial resources are and how to access them. Often, bank accounts, investments, and savings are spread across multiple institutions, and without a clear record, it can become a daunting and time-consuming task for the family to gather this information. The uncertainty and confusion that come from not knowing what accounts exist or how to access them can add immense stress during an already emotionally challenging time.

By keeping everything documented in one central place—whether it's bank accounts, investments, loans, or insurance policies—you ensure that your family has a straightforward roadmap to follow. Additionally, it is crucial to specify the nominations for these accounts clearly. Nominees are individuals designated to receive the funds or manage the accounts in your absence, which helps prevent legal complications and disputes among family members. Properly documenting both the account details and the nominated beneficiaries ensures that your family can smoothly access these resources, avoiding delays, unnecessary paperwork, and financial hardships. This not only prevents confusion but also provides them with the peace of mind that they can manage and secure their future without unnecessary complications.

Story 1: Priya and the Missing Bank Accounts

Priya, a mother of two, was living her life like many of us do—working hard, raising her children, and trusting that her husband, Rajesh, had everything under control when it came to their finances. But one tragic morning, her world was turned upside down when Rajesh suddenly passed away due to a heart attack. In the weeks that followed, Priya faced a challenge she never anticipated. She knew they had bank accounts and investments, but she didn't know how many, where they were, or how to access them.

Priya spent months going through old papers, calling banks, and trying to figure out where their money was. Some accounts were with a local bank, others were with financial institutions she had never even heard of. She discovered savings accounts, fixed deposits, and investments that had gone untouched for years—all of which she had no idea existed.

If Rajesh had organized their finances properly, it would have been a completely different story. He could have listed their bank accounts, including the account numbers, login information, and branch details, all in one place. Instead of scrambling in the midst of her grief, Priya could have accessed everything smoothly and without stress.

Key Takeaway:

As the Family CEO, it's crucial to keep all your **bank accounts, investments, loans, savings,** and **fixed deposits** in one secure and organized location. This way, your family will know where everything is, making a difficult time less stressful.

Action Step:

- Create a financial portfolio with all your account details, including:
- Bank account numbers and branch details.
- Login credentials for online banking.
- Investment details (mutual funds, stocks, bonds).
- Fixed deposit amounts and maturity dates.
- Outstanding loans and repayment schedules.

Story 2: Ankit's Complex Real Estate Inheritance

Ankit's father, Mr. Mehra, was a successful businessman who had invested in several properties over the years. Mr. Mehra was proud of his portfolio—he owned the family home in Delhi, a rental apartment in Mumbai, and a small farmhouse in Shimla. But he made one mistake: he never told anyone about the details of his real estate investments. He thought his children would figure it out later. But when Mr. Mehra suddenly passed away, Ankit and his siblings had no idea what properties he owned, which were rented out, or even who the tenants were.

For months, they tried to track down property deeds, loan documents, and rental agreements. They spent significant time and money on legal fees to gather all the necessary documents. The properties were in different cities, and none of the siblings had experience in managing real estate. If their father had simply documented the details of his properties—where they were, the status of any loans or mortgages, and who was renting them—it would have been a much smoother process.

Key Takeaway:

As the Family CEO, you need to document every detail about your family's **real estate holdings**. That includes property addresses, ownership documents, loan details, rental agreements, and any other relevant information. Your family should never be left guessing.

Action Step:

Create a Real Estate Folder containing:

- Property addresses and current market values.
- Ownership documents (deeds, titles).
- Loan or mortgage information (outstanding amounts, lender contact details).
- Tenant details and rental agreements (if applicable).

Story 3: Suman and the Forgotten Valuables

Suman was known for her love of collecting traditional jewelry and artwork. Over the years, she had accumulated a beautiful collection that she was proud of. However, after her passing, her children were left confused. Some of her jewelry was in a bank locker, while other pieces were kept in different places around the house. No one knew the exact value of her collection, and Suman had never documented what should go to whom.

To make things worse, they found out later that some of the pieces had lost their insurance coverage because Suman had forgotten to renew the policies. The family spent months trying to locate all the valuables, having pieces appraised, and deciding how to divide them. This could have been avoided if Suman had simply listed her jewelry, artwork, and other valuables in an inventory and noted their locations.

Key Takeaway:

It's important to create an **Inventory of Valuables** for all your high-value items, including jewelry, artwork, vehicles, and any other collectibles. Knowing where these items are stored and their insurance status is crucial to ensuring they're properly managed after you're gone.

Action Step: Create a Valuables Log with-

- A detailed list of items (jewelry, artwork, vehicles).
- Appraisal values for each item.
- Insurance policy details (renewal dates, coverage amounts).
- Storage locations (home, bank lockers, safes).

Reflecting on Your Own Situation:

Imagine yourself in Priya's, Ankit's, or Suman's shoes. What would happen to your family if they had to deal with this kind of confusion and stress? Do they know where your accounts are, what properties you own, or what valuables you've collected over the years?

Take a moment to ask yourself:

- If something were to happen to me tomorrow, would my family know how to access all our bank accounts, investments, and real estate?
- Is there an easy-to-read document that they can refer to, or would they be left scrambling, like Priya or Ankit's family?

Tip 1: List all bank accounts, including savings, checking, and investment accounts, along with the institution name, account number, and balance.

Tip 2: Regularly update your portfolio with new investments or any changes to existing accounts to keep information current.

Tip 3: Store login credentials securely using a password manager, and make sure a trusted person has access.

Financial Portfolio Tracker

Category	Details (Fill it with a blue or black pen)
Bank Accounts	
Bank Name	Enter bank name
Account Number	Enter account number
Branch/IFSC Code	Enter branch details
Account Type	(Savings/Checking/Fixed)
Current Balance	Enter balance
Beneficiary Name	Enter nominee/beneficiary details
Access Information	Enter login credentials or PIN (optional)
Investments	
Investment Type	(Mutual Funds/Stocks/Bonds/Fixed Deposit etc.)
Provider Name	Enter provider name
Investment Account	Enter account number or policy number
Maturity Date	Enter the maturity date if applicable
Investment Value	Enter current value
Beneficiary	Enter nominee details
Loans	
Loan Type	(Home Loan/Car Loan/Personal Loan, etc.)
Loan Provider	Enter loan provider name, etc.
Loan Account Number	Enter the loan account number
Remaining Balance	Enter the outstanding loan amount
Monthly Payment	Enter EMI amount
Payment Due Date	Enter the date
Cryptocurrency Holdings	
Crypto Wallet Provider	Enter the name of the crypto wallet service or exchange
Wallet Address	Enter the public address of the cryptocurrency wallet
Cryptocurrency Type	Specify the type of cryptocurrency (e.g., Bitcoin, Ethereum)
Total Crypto Bal	Enter the total value of cryptocurrency held in wallet

Private Key Location	Specify the location where the private keys are stored
2FA Enabled	Yes/No; specify how to access 2FA if applicable
Backup Seed Phrase Location	Specify the physical or digital location of the seed/recovery phrase
Exchange Account Details	Exchange account details where cryptocurrencies are held
Beneficiary	Enter the name of the beneficiary for the crypto holdings

Actionable Steps:

- Fill in all your financial account details to provide a complete overview.
- Update balances and maturity dates periodically to keep this document current.
- Ensure this template is easily accessible to your spouse or trusted family members.

Cryptocurrency Holdings:

Store wallet addresses, private keys, and recovery phrases in a secure location (physical or digital) and ensure trusted family members have access to these details.

"*My mother owned several properties in Goa, but after she passed, the lack of clear documentation caused endless legal delays. If we had something like Family CEO to organize property titles and mortgage details, we could have managed everything smoothly and avoided the legal hassles.*"

- Vanessa D'Souza, Goa.

Chapter 2: Securing Real Estate and Property

Why It Matters: Real estate is often one of the most valuable assets a family owns, but it can also become the most complicated to manage, especially after the sudden loss of a family member. If property titles, deeds, mortgage details, or rental agreements aren't clearly organized, it can lead to confusion, misunderstandings, or even legal disputes. In the worst cases, family members may end up facing long legal battles, which can be both emotionally and financially draining, or risk losing ownership due to a lack of documentation.

By keeping a clear and comprehensive record of all property-related information—including ownership documents, mortgage terms, rental agreements, and any other pertinent details—you ensure that your family knows exactly what properties are owned, the status of each, and how to proceed if any decisions need to be made. This not only simplifies the process of managing real estate but also protects the value of the assets, ensuring that your family's legacy is preserved and passed on without complications or delays.

Real-Life Example:

1. In 2017, a widow from California struggled for over two years to secure her late husband's property. The husband, a successful entrepreneur, had owned multiple properties across different states. However, he hadn't clearly documented the details of his real estate holdings. His widow had to battle legal issues because some deeds were missing, and the mortgages on a couple of properties were in default without her knowledge. Had there been proper documentation, she could have settled the estate smoothly without lengthy legal disputes.

2. Amar's father, Mr. Ramesh, owned two properties in Chennai, but after his sudden passing, Amar struggled to find the documents proving ownership. One house had a pending mortgage, and the other

had tenants. Without the proper paperwork, Amar faced weeks of delays and legal complications. If his father had kept everything together, it would have saved Amar a lot of stress and time.

Actionable Steps:

- Complete all sections for each property you own.
- Keep documents (deeds, rental agreements) attached to this checklist.
- Update the current market value annually and review mortgage terms regularly.

These templates are designed to help families stay organized and ensure that all financial, real estate, and valuable assets are accounted for. By utilizing **FamilyCEO.in**, users can easily fill in these templates online and keep everything up-to-date and accessible for their family members when needed.

Tip 1: Document property details such as title documents, mortgage agreements, and ownership percentages for each property.

Tip 2: If properties are rented, include tenant details and lease agreements to ensure continuity.

Tip 3: Update property valuations periodically to maintain an accurate record of assets.

Real Estate Information Tracker

Property Type	Details (Fill it with a blue or black pen)
Primary Property	
Property Address	Enter the address
Ownership Documents	Deed, Title, Ownership papers
Current Market Value	Enter estimated market value
Mortgage Information	Enter mortgage provider, loan number, outstanding balance
Mortgage Repayment Terms	Monthly payment amount, due date
Nominee Details	Enter nominee for the property
Rental Property	
Property Address	Enter the address
Rental Agreement	Attach a copy for details
Tenant Contact Information	Enter tenant's name and contact details
Lease Terms	Monthly rental amount, due date, provision date
Ownership Documents	Deed, Title, Ownership papers
Mortgage Information	Enter mortgage details if applicable
Vacation Home	
Property Address	Enter the address
Ownership Documents	Deed, Title, Ownership papers
Current Market Value	Enter estimated market value
Mortgage Information	Enter mortgage provider, loan number, outstanding balance
Property Maintenance Plan	Enter any details on upkeep responsibilities

Personal Notes

Chapter 3: Safeguarding Valuables and Physical Assets

Preserving Family's Assets such as jewelry, cars, or cherished family heirlooms, is crucial to maintaining both financial and sentimental value for future generations. However, without proper documentation, these valuables can easily become a source of confusion, disputes, or even unintentional loss. Family members may not be aware of the full extent of what has been kept, where these items are stored, or who they were meant for, which can lead to misunderstandings and potential conflicts during an already difficult time.

By documenting all valuable items—such as creating an inventory with descriptions, photographs, estimated values, and locations—you can ensure that your family knows exactly what is owned and how it should be managed. Including specific details, like who the intended recipient is or where the items are stored (e.g., bank lockers, safes, or secure locations), will provide clarity and prevent disputes. This not only helps protect the financial worth of these assets but also ensures that sentimental items are passed down as intended, preserving your family's heritage and providing comfort in times of loss.

Real-Life Example:

1) A case in the UK in 2015 highlighted the importance of safeguarding valuables. A man who had a significant collection of rare artwork and family heirlooms passed away unexpectedly. Unfortunately, he hadn't left a detailed inventory of his valuable possessions, and his family didn't know the exact location of some items. They later discovered that several pieces had been misplaced or sold without their knowledge. With no documentation, it became almost impossible to trace some of the missing items. The family's lawyer recommended creating a detailed inventory of valuables to prevent this kind of loss.

2) When Yusuf passed away, his wife Fatima didn't know where he had stored the family jewelry. There was a locker at the bank, but she couldn't find the key.

They also had a car in Yusuf's name, but the documents were missing. Fatima had to spend months sorting out the mess, which could have been avoided if Yusuf had documented these valuables clearly.

Actionable Steps:

- Document every valuable item in your possession.
- Include appraisals and insurance details for easy reference.
- Regularly update storage locations and appraisal values.

These templates are designed to help families stay organized and ensure that all financial, real estate, and valuable assets are accounted for.

Inventory Template Tracker for Valuables

Item	Details (Fill it with a blue or black pen)
Jewelry	
Item Description	Gold necklace, diamond ring, etc.
Appraisal Value	Enter appraised value
Storage	Home safe, bank locker, etc.
Insurance Policy	Insurance details, policy number, and expiration date
Beneficiary	Nominee or family member to receive the item
Vehicles	
Vehicle Type	Car, motorcycle, etc.
Make & Model	Enter make and model
Purchase Year	Enter year
Current Value	Enter estimated current value
Insurance Details	Insurance policy number, provider, and expiration date
Registration	Vehicle registration details
Beneficiary	Nominee or family member to receive the vehicle
Art Collectibles	
Items	Painting, sculpture, rare book, etc.
Artist/Creator	Artist or creator's name
Appraisal	Enter appraised value
Storage	Home safe, gallery, etc.
Insurance Policy	Insurance details, policy number, and expiration date
Beneficiary	Nominee or family member to receive the item

Tip 1: Take photos of high-value items (e.g., jewelry, art) and attach appraisal certificates to document their worth.
Tip 2: Record where each item is stored (home safe, bank locker) and share access instructions with a trusted person.
Tip 3: Note any insurance policies covering valuable items and ensure the policies are up-to-date.

Chapter 4: Managing Warranties and Guarantees

"DON'T LET YOUR FAMILY FACE AVOIDABLE COSTS— KEEP WARRANTIES HANDY SO THEY CAN TAKE CARE OF EVERYTHING YOU LEFT BEHIND."

Overview: Expensive products, such as electronics, appliances, vehicles, and other high-value items, often come with warranties or guarantees that protect the owner from unexpected repair or replacement costs. However, without proper documentation of these warranties, the benefits they offer can be easily overlooked or forgotten. Losing track of the warranty period, coverage details, or the required paperwork can result in missed opportunities to save money, forcing family members to pay out of pocket for repairs or replacements that could have been covered.

By keeping a detailed record of all warranties and guarantees—including the type of coverage, expiration dates, terms, and contact details for service— families can ensure that any necessary repairs or replacements are handled smoothly and without hassle. This not only saves time and money but also provides peace of mind, knowing that valuable assets are properly maintained and protected. A well-organized warranty tracker ensures that your family has everything they need to make claims efficiently, safeguarding these assets and reducing unnecessary financial burdens.

Real-Life Example:

1. In 2018, a family in Germany faced financial difficulties after their home appliances, purchased two years earlier, stopped working. The father had passed away, and the mother couldn't locate the warranties or guarantees for several expensive products, including their refrigerator and washing machine. Without these documents, the family had to bear the full repair costs. If the father had kept a record of all warranties, the family could have claimed repairs or replacements free of charge, saving them significant costs during a difficult time.

2. When Vivek's refrigerator broke down six months after his death, his family had no idea it was still under warranty. They ended up paying for a costly repair, unaware that the warranty could have covered it. A quick note of the warranty information would have saved money.

Actionable Steps:

1. Complete this template for all high-value items with warranties and guarantees.
2. Ensure documents such as receipts and warranty cards are stored in a secure location (physical or digital).
3. Set reminders for warranty expiration dates and renewals where necessary.

Tip 1: Keep original receipts and warranty cards in a designated place for easy access.

Tip 2: Set reminders for warranty expiration dates to ensure repairs or replacements are done within coverage.

Tip 3: Update the tracker with new purchases immediately to keep records current.

Warranties & Guarantees Tracker for High-Value Products

Product Type	Details (Fill it with a blue or black pen)
Appliance	
Item Description	Refrigerator, Washing Machine, Air Conditioner, etc.
Brand	Enter brand name
Model/Serial Number	Enter model and serial number
Purchase Date	Enter the date of purchase
Warranty Expiration Date	Enter the warranty end date
Guarantee Information	Enter any guarantee details
Service Center Contact	Enter the contact details of the service center
Warranty Coverage Details	List the coverage (parts, labor, specific items)
Storage Location for Documents	Home folder, cloud storage, etc.
Electronics	
Item Description	Television, Laptop, Mobile Phone, etc.
Brand	Enter brand name
Model/Serial Number	Enter model and serial number
Purchase Date	Enter the date of purchase
Warranty Expiration Date	Enter the warranty end date
Guarantee Information	Enter any guarantee details
Service Center Contact	Enter the contact details of the service center
Warranty Coverage Details	List the coverage (parts, labor, specific items)
Storage Location	Home folder, cloud storage, etc.
Furniture	
Item Description	Sofa set, Dining table, Desk, etc.
Brand/Manufacturer	Enter manufacturer details
Purchase Date	Enter the date of purchase
Warranty Expiration Date	Enter the warranty end date
Guarantee Information	Enter any guarantee details

Service Center Contact	Enter the contact details of the service center
Warranty Coverage Details	List the coverage - parts, service, specific terms
Storage Location for Documents	Home folder, cloud storage, etc.
Vehicles	
Vehicle Description	Car, Bike, Scooter, etc.
Make & Model	Enter make and model
Purchase Date	Enter the date of purchase
Warranty Expiration Date	Enter the warranty end date
Guarantee Information	Enter any guarantee details
Service Center Contact	Enter the contact details of the service center
Warranty Coverage Details	List the coverage - parts, service, specific terms
Storage Location for Documents	Home folder, cloud storage, etc.
Other High-Value Products	
Item Description	High-end camera, luxury item, electronics
Brand	Enter the brand name
Model/Serial Number	Enter model and serial number
Purchase Date	Enter the date of purchase
Warranty Expiration Date	Enter the warranty end date
Guarantee Information	Enter any guarantee details
Service Center Contact	Enter the contact details of the service center
Warranty Coverage Details	List the coverage - parts, labor, specific terms
Storage Location for Documents	Home folder, cloud storage, etc.

Personal Notes

Chapter 5: Documenting Liabilities and Financial Commitments

"DOCUMENTING LIABILITIES TODAY HELPS PREVENT FINANCIAL BURDENS FROM BECOMING OVERWHELMING FOR YOUR FAMILY TOMORROW."

Overview: Understanding and settling outstanding debts such as loans, mortgages, credit card balances, or any other liabilities is crucial, especially after the sudden loss of a family head. Without proper documentation, family members may find it difficult to track the different loans and their repayment schedules, leading to missed payments, penalties, and potential legal issues. Unsettled liabilities can put an immense financial burden on the family, adding to the emotional stress they are already experiencing.

By using a **Liabilities Tracker**, you can ensure that all debts are clearly documented—including the type of liability, lender information, outstanding amounts, repayment schedules, and due dates. This helps the family be aware of any pending payments, settle debts on time, and avoid penalties or negative consequences. It also provides a clear overview of the family's financial obligations, allowing them to make informed decisions and manage their finances responsibly. Keeping track of liabilities not only reduces confusion but also allows for a more organized approach to financial management, ensuring the family remains financially stable even in challenging times.

Real-Life Example:

1) A man in Australia passed away suddenly, leaving behind a personal loan and a mortgage that his family knew nothing about. The lender soon began calling his widow, demanding repayment. The family had no record of the debt and was unprepared for the financial burden. Eventually, the bank agreed to extend the repayment period, but it took months of negotiation. If the deceased had properly documented his liabilities, his family could have settled the debts more efficiently and without emotional stress.

2) A woman in Canada passed away unexpectedly, leaving her adult children unaware of several financial commitments she had made. Among these was a business loan she had co-signed

for a friend, which her children only learned about when they received legal notices demanding repayment. The children also discovered an outstanding car loan and a credit card with a substantial balance. Without clear documentation of these liabilities, the family faced significant delays in addressing the debts, and they even risked legal action from creditors. By the time everything was sorted out, the financial and emotional toll was overwhelming. Had she documented these liabilities clearly, her family could have been prepared, avoiding unnecessary stress and ensuring that her obligations were managed smoothly and respectfully.

Actionable Steps:

- List all your liabilities, including mortgages, car loans, personal loans, and credit card debts.

- Ensure all loan documents and account details are stored in a secure, easy-to-access location for family members.

- Regularly update the outstanding balances and repayment schedules to keep this document current.

Tip 1: Document loan agreements and payment schedules for all outstanding debts, including credit cards and mortgages.

Tip 2: Review and update the tracker whenever there is a change in loan terms, such as interest rates.

Tip 3: Include repayment plans or strategies for clearing liabilities in case of emergencies.

Liabilities Tracker for Mortgages, Loans, and Debt Repayment Plans

Liability Type	Details (Fill it with a blue or black pen)
Mortgage	
Property Address	Enter the address of the property
Loan Provider	Enter the name of the bank/lender
Loan Account Number	Enter loan account number
Loan Start Date	Enter the start date of the mortgage
Loan Amount	Enter the total loan amount
Current Outstanding Balance	Enter the remaining balance on the mortgage
Monthly Repayment	Enter the EMI amount
Loan Repayment Due Date	Enter the due date for the next payment
Interest Rate	Enter the interest rate
Mortgage Documents Location	Physical storage or digital storage location
Beneficiary/Heir Information	Enter the nominee or beneficiary
Car Loan	
Vehicle Make & Model	Enter make and model of the vehicle
Loan Provider	Enter the name of the bank/lender
Loan Account Number	Enter loan account number
Loan Start Date	Enter the start date of the car loan
Loan Amount	Enter the total loan amount
Current Outstanding Balance	Enter the remaining balance on the car loan
Monthly Repayment Amount	Enter the EMI amount
Loan Repayment Due Date	Enter the due date for the next payment
Interest Rate	Enter the interest rate
Loan Documents Location	Physical storage or digital storage location
Beneficiary/Heir Information	Enter the nominee or beneficiary
Personal Loan	
Loan Provider	Enter the name of the bank/lender
Loan Account Number	Enter loan account number

Loan Start Date	Enter the start date of the personal loan
Loan Amount	Enter the total loan amount
Current Outstanding Balance	Enter the remaining balance on the personal loan
Monthly Repayment Amount	Enter the EMI amount
Loan Repayment Due Date	Enter the due date for the next payment
Interest Rate	Enter the interest rate
Loan Documents Location	Physical storage or digital storage location
Beneficiary/Heir Information	Enter the nominee or beneficiary
Credit Card Debt	
Credit Card Issuer	Enter the name of the bank or credit issuer
Credit Card Number	Enter the last four digits on the card
Outstanding Balance	Enter the remaining balance on the card
Monthly Payment Due Date	Enter the due date for the next payment
Minimum Payment Due	Enter the minimum payment required
Interest Rate	Enter the interest rate on the credit card
Card Documents Location	Physical storage or digital storage location
Beneficiary/Heir Information	Enter the nominee or beneficiary
Other Loans or Debts	
Loan/ Debt Type	Enter the type of loan or debt
Loan Provider	Enter the name of the bank/lender
Loan Account Number	Enter loan account number
Loan Start Date	Enter the start date of the loan
Loan Amount	Enter the total loan amount
Current Outstanding Balance	Enter the remaining balance
Monthly Repayment Amount	Enter the EMI amount
Loan Repayment Due Date	Enter the due date for the next payment
Interest Rate	Enter the interest rate
Loan Documents Location	Physical storage or digital storage location
Beneficiary/Heir Information	Enter the nominee or beneficiary

Personal Notes

"Even in my case, I am still compiling and struggling to organize all my family's insurance details, including Mediclaim, term insurance, mutual funds, SIPs, equity, loan liabilities, and other assets in one place. When I began planning for my child's future education, I realized just how scattered all my documents were - school fees, savings plans, scholarships. If I had something like Family CEO to help organize these details, it would have provided me with peace of mind, knowing everything was in order."

- Abhijit Gujarati, Nashik.

Chapter 6: Securing Children's Education

"A WELL-DOCUMENTED EDUCATION PLAN TODAY IS THE FOUNDATION FOR YOUR CHILDREN'S BRIGHTER TOMORROW."

Overview: Planning and documenting education-related expenses, such as school fees, overseas education plans, hostel charges, or long-term savings for education, is essential to secure your children's future. When the head of the family is no longer present, the uncertainty surrounding how educational expenses will be managed can cause significant disruption to the child's learning journey. Ensuring that all education-related information is clearly documented provides your family with a clear financial pathway to follow.

By creating a detailed record of all current and future educational expenses, including any long-term savings or scholarships planned for your children, you ensure their education continues without interruption. This not only helps your family manage these costs efficiently but also provides peace of mind, knowing that your children will have access to the resources they need to pursue their goals, even if you are not there to guide them personally. Proper documentation is key to making sure your children's education remains a priority and that they have the support they need to achieve their dreams.

Real-Life Example:

In 2019, a family in Mumbai, India, faced a sudden crisis when the father, who had been saving for his children's overseas education, passed away. Unfortunately, he hadn't shared the details of the education savings plans with his wife. The children's future education was put at risk as the mother scrambled to locate the savings and figure out how to manage the expenses. After a months-long search, she finally found the documents, but by then, they had already missed important application deadlines. Documenting the savings and education plans could have prevented this uncertainty.

Actionable Steps:
- List all important details about your child's education, including tuition fees, payment schedules, and overseas education plans.

- Keep all documents related to school fees, hostel charges, and overseas education in one secure location, either physically or digitally.
- Update the template regularly with fee receipts, payment due dates, and any changes in educational plans

Children's Education Information Tracker

Education Category	Details (Fill it with a blue or black pen)
Child's Name	Enter child's full name
Date of Birth	Enter child's date of birth
Current School/College	Enter the name of the school or college
Class/Grade	Enter the current class or grade
School Address	Enter the school's address
School Contact Information	Enter the school's phone number and email
School Fees	
Annual Tuition Fees	Enter the total annual tuition fees
Payment Frequency	(Monthly/Quarterly/Yearly)
Next Payment Due Date	Enter the next due date for school fees
Amount Due	Enter the amount due for the next payment
Payment Method	Specify the method of payment (bank transfer, cheque, etc.)
Documents Location	Physical or digital location of fee receipts and tax systems
Hostel Charges	
Hostel Name (if applicable)	Enter the hostel's name
Monthly/Annual Hostel Fee	Enter the monthly or annual hostel fees
Payment Frequency	(Monthly/Quarterly/Yearly)
Next Payment Due Date	Enter the next due date for hostel charges
Amount Due	Enter the amount due for the next payment

Payment Method	Specify the method of payment (e.g. bank transfer, cheque, etc.)
Hostel Contact Information	Enter the hostel's phone number and email
Overseas Education Plans	
Intended Country of Study	Enter the country where your child plans to study
Estimated Annual Tuition Fees	Enter the estimated tuition fees for the program
Estimated Living Costs	Enter the estimated cost of living in the country
Scholarships/Financial Aid	List any scholarships or financial aid available or applied for
Start Date of Program	Enter the expected start date
Visa and Documentation	Specify the status of visa applications and necessary documents
Documents Location	Physical or digital location of application documents
Savings for Education	
Education Fund Name	Enter the name of any education savings plan or fund
Fund Provider	Enter the name of the financial institution or provider
Account Number	Enter the account number
Current Balance	Enter the current balance in the education fund
Beneficiary Name	Enter the beneficiary's name for the education fund
Maturity Date (if applicable)	Enter the maturity date of the education fund

Personal Notes

Tip 1: Keep a record of tuition fees, scholarships, and educational savings plans.

Tip 2: Note any upcoming school or university application deadlines to stay prepared.

Tip 3: Include future education plans, such as overseas study aspirations, with estimated costs.

, When my husband needed emergency care, I couldn't find his health insurance information and ended up paying out of pocket for treatments. A resource like Family CEO, where all medical and insurance details are kept securely in one place, would have made the process so much easier."

- Pradnya More, Goregaon.

Chapter 7: Health, Insurance, and Medical Records

"HAVING YOUR HEALTH INSURANCE AND MEDICAL RECORDS DOCUMENTED TODAY COULD BE THE LIFELINE YOUR FAMILY NEEDS IN TIMES OF CRISIS."

Overview:

Health insurance and medical records are essential for effectively managing healthcare expenses, especially during emergencies. Without organized information, accessing the right medical care or knowing the benefits available through insurance can become a stressful and overwhelming task for your family. Having clear documentation ensures that your loved ones can quickly access important details such as policy numbers, network hospitals, coverage limits, and ongoing treatments without confusion or delays.

Additionally, knowing about healthcare tie-ups, such as employer-provided insurance or discounts through professional associations, can significantly reduce medical costs. For example, being aware of discounts or special agreements with hospitals could save your family a substantial amount during a time when every moment and every rupee counts. By keeping a detailed record of all health insurance policies, ongoing treatments, and relevant medical contacts, you empower your family to make informed healthcare decisions and ensure that they receive the best possible care without unnecessary financial burden. Proper documentation can be a critical difference in ensuring quick and efficient healthcare access in times of need.

Moreover, if you have decided to bank your child's **umbilical cord blood**, keeping track of these records is vital. This information could provide invaluable health benefits in the future, such as treatments involving stem cells for serious medical conditions. Clear documentation of the cord blood banking contract, storage location, and contact information is crucial to ensuring that these potential resources are accessible when needed.

Real-Life Example:

1. A family in Canada experienced a medical emergency when the father suffered a stroke. He had a health insurance policy that covered most of his treatments, but his wife and children were

unaware of the coverage details. They ended up paying for treatments out of pocket, only to discover months later that they could have claimed reimbursement through the policy. Had the father documented his insurance policies and medical records, the family could have avoided this financial burden and managed his healthcare more efficiently.

2. The author himself, a chartered accountant, experienced this firsthand. He wasn't aware that his professional body, the Western India Regional Council (WIRC) of the CA institute, had a tie-up with a well-known hospital. As a result, he ended up paying the full amount for his spouse's hospitalization, missing out on a potential 20% discount on several components of the medical bill. Had he known and documented this tie-up, it would have reduced the financial burden significantly. This example highlights the importance of documenting health insurance policies, medical records, and professional benefits to ensure you take full advantage of the available resources.

3. Another example involves **umbilical cord blood banking**. A couple in the United States decided to bank their newborn's umbilical cord blood, recognizing the potential health benefits it could offer in the future. Unfortunately, they did not document the details or keep track of the bank's contact information. When their child was diagnosed with a health condition that could have benefited from stem cell therapy, they faced challenges in locating the storage bank. Proper documentation of these records would have allowed them to access the necessary information without any delays.

Professional Membership Tie-Ups:

- **Professional Body Name**: Enter the name of the professional organization (e.g., Chartered Accountants Association).

- **Hospital Tie-Up Details**: List the hospitals or healthcare providers that have special tie-ups with the professional body.

- **Benefits/Discounts Available**: Mention the specific benefits available, such as discounts on hospitalization, consultations, or medical procedures.

- **Contact Information**: Provide the contact person or department responsible for assisting with hospital tie-ups.

- **Documents Location**: Physical or digital location of documents verifying eligibility for benefits (e.g., membership ID).

Umbilical Cord Blood Banking:

- **Banking Agreement**: Copy of the contract with the cord blood bank.

- **Storage Location**: Details of where the umbilical cord blood is stored.

- **Contact Information**: Contact details for the cord blood bank.

- **Banking Duration and Renewal**: Information regarding the duration of storage and any renewal dates.

Actionable Steps:

- Fill in all relevant details for each family member, including medical history, insurance information, and emergency instructions.

- Keep digital copies of medical insurance policies, claim instructions, **umbilical cord blood banking** records, and important health records in one secure, accessible location.

- Regularly update this template with new treatments, health changes, policy renewals, and cord blood banking information.

Health & Medical Information Template

Category	Details (Fill it with a blue or black pen)
Family Member Information	
Name	Enter the family member's full name
Date of Birth	Enter the family member's date of birth
Blood Type	Enter blood type
Known Allergies	List any known allergies
Chronic Conditions	List any chronic medical conditions, such as diabetes or others
Current Medications	List current medications and dosages

Primary Doctor Contact	Doctor's name, contact number and address
Medical Insurance	
Insurance Provider	Enter the name of the insurance company
Policy Number	List the policy number
Coverage Details	List coverage information - inpatient, outpatient, dental, etc.
Insurance Start Date	Enter the start date of the policy
Expiration Date	Enter the expiration date of the policy
Monthly Premium	Enter the monthly premium amount
Claim Process	Brief instructions for filing a claim, documents required
Insurance Agent Contact	Enter the insurance agent's name and contact number
Insurance Documents Location	Physical or digital location where you keep policy documents
Emergency Instructions	
Emergency Contact Name	Enter the name of the person to contact in an emergency
Emergency Contact Phone	Enter their phone number
Preferred Hospital	Enter the preferred hospital or clinic
Special Medical Instructions	Any specific emergency instructions, e.g. requires insulin
Location of Medical Records	Physical or digital location of medical records
Family History	
Family Member Name	Enter family member's name
Known Medical Conditions	List any significant hereditary conditions in the family
Past Surgeries	List any major surgeries or medical interventions
Immunization Records	List vaccinations, including dates
General Health Summary	Provide a brief overview of the family member's overall health

Ongoing Treatments	
Family Member Name	Enter family member's name
Condition Being Treated	Describe the condition being treated
Doctor/Physician Contact	Doctor's name, phone number, and address
Treatment Plan	Describe the ongoing treatment plan and medications
Frequency of Treatment	Specify the frequency of treatment or appointments
Next Appointment Date	Enter the date of the next appointment
Documents Location	Physical or digital location of treatment records
Professional Membership Tie-Ups	
Professional Body Name	Enter the name of the professional organization
Hospital Tie-Up Details	List the hospitals or healthcare providers that have special tie-ups with the professional body
Benefits/Discounts Available	Mention the specific benefits available such as discounts on hospitalization, consultations, or medical procedures
Contact Information	Provide the contact person or department responsible for assisting with hospital tie-ups
Documents Location	Physical or digital location of documents verifying eligibility for benefits (e.g., membership IDs)
Umbilical Cord Blood Banking	
Banking Agreement	Copy of the contract with the cord blood bank
Storage Location	Details of where the umbilical cord blood is stored
Contact Information	Contact details for the cord blood bank
Banking Duration and Renewal	Information regarding the duration of storage and any renewal fees

Tip 1: Document all health insurance policies, including coverage details, claim procedures, and emergency contacts.

Tip 2: Keep a copy of important medical records and prescriptions, and update them periodically.

Tip 3: If there are healthcare tie-ups, note the benefits and provide contact details for verification.

"*When my brother passed, we struggled to access his online accounts and digital assets. If we had a tool like Family CEO to document passwords and account details, it would have saved us from weeks of frustration trying to sort everything out.*"

- *Rajesh Dubey, Kolkata.*

Chapter 8: Managing Digital Assets

"YOUR ONLINE WORLD IS AS REAL AS ANYTHING ELSE; MAKE SURE YOUR LOVED ONES HAVE THE KEYS TO UNLOCK IT WHEN THE TIME COMES."

Overview: In today's digital world, managing online accounts, cryptocurrencies, and other digital assets is as important as managing physical assets. Digital assets can include everything from financial accounts like cryptocurrencies, online investment portfolios, and digital wallets to more personal assets like social media accounts, cloud storage, and subscription services. Without proper documentation and secure record-keeping, these digital assets can become inaccessible in the event of a sudden loss, causing significant financial and sentimental loss for the family.

Ensuring that all necessary information, such as usernames, passwords, encryption keys, and access instructions, is properly recorded helps prevent these valuable assets from being lost. Without this documentation, your loved ones may not be able to access funds, cancel subscriptions, or take control of important online services, leaving these assets vulnerable or entirely unreachable. By documenting everything in one secure location, you empower your family to take timely action, minimize losses, and ensure a seamless transition of control over these digital assets. Properly managed digital assets also provide continuity, whether it's transferring cryptocurrency funds or securing important memories stored online.

Real-Life Examples:
1. After Gaurav's death, his wife Rashmi was overwhelmed by ongoing subscription renewals for accounts she couldn't access. If Gaurav had documented his digital assets, Rashmi could have canceled the subscriptions immediately.

2. In 2020, an American business owner passed away unexpectedly, leaving behind a thriving online business. His widow didn't have access to the login information for his business accounts, social media, or email, which were crucial for continuing the company's operations. Without proper documentation of digital assets, she had to hire cybersecurity experts to recover access, which delayed business activities and caused revenue

losses. A simple digital asset tracker could have provided the necessary information to ensure a smoother transition.

3. One of the most infamous cases involving digital assets occurred in 2018, when the founder of **QuadrigaCX**, a Canadian cryptocurrency exchange, Gerald Cotten, passed away suddenly. He was the only person with the passwords and encryption keys to access the exchange's cold wallets, where cryptocurrency worth over **$190 million** was stored. After his death, thousands of customers lost access to their funds because there was no backup plan or way to retrieve the information. The incident left customers with no way to access their investments, causing financial havoc and leading to legal battles. This case highlights the critical importance of documenting digital assets securely and ensuring that trusted individuals have access in case of emergencies.

Actionable Steps:
- Fill in details for all your online accounts, including email, social media, banking, and subscription services.
- Store login credentials, passwords, and security questions securely, and enable two-factor authentication wherever possible.
- Regularly update the template with changes to passwords, account renewals, or new subscriptions.
- Specify instructions for how to manage or close online accounts in case of your passing.

Tip 1: Record login details for all important digital accounts, including social media, banking, and email.

Tip 2: Use a password manager to store credentials securely, and provide access instructions for trusted individuals.

Tip 3: Update the tracker whenever you change a password or open a new account.

Digital Assets & Online Accounts Tracker

Category	Details (Fill it with a blue or black pen)
Email Accounts	
Email Provider	Enter the email provider (e.g. Gmail, Yahoo)
Email Address	Enter the email address
Password	Enter the password
Security Questions	List security questions and answers
Two-Factor Authentication	Enabled/Disabled, instructions to access
Backup Email/Phone	Enter backup email or phone number for recovery
Documents Location	Physical or digital location for backup codes
Social Media Accounts	
Platform Name	Enter the name of the platform (e.g. Facebook, Instagram)
Username/Email	Enter the username or email linked to the account
Password	Enter the password
Account Deletion Instructions	Instructions for deleting the account after passing
Two-Factor Authentication	Enabled/Disabled, instructions to access
Backup Email/Phone	Enter the backup email or phone number for recovery
Documents Location	Physical or digital location for account details
Banking & Financial Accounts	
Bank Name	Enter the name of the bank
Online Banking Username	Enter username for online banking
Password	Enter the password
Two-Factor Authentication	Enabled/Disabled, instructions to access
Security Questions	List security questions and answers
Backup Email/Phone	Enter backup email or phone number for recovery
Documents Location	Physical or digital location for banking details

Cloud Storage Accounts	
Cloud Storage Provider	Enter the provider (e.g., Google Drive, Dropbox)
Username/Email	Enter the username or email used for the account
Password	Enter the password
Two-Factor Authentication	Enable/disable instructions to access
Backup Email/Phone	Enter backup email or phone number for recovery
Documents Location	Physical or digital location for access codes and accounts
Subscription Services	
Service Name	Enter the service (e.g., Netflix, Spotify)
Username/Email	Enter the username or email associated with the service
Password	Enter the password
Renewal Date	Enter the renewal date or payment schedule
Payment Method	Enter the linked payment method for the service
Subscription Details	Enter the plan details (e.g., Family, Premium)
Cancellation Instructions	Enter instructions on how to cancel the subscription
Documents Location	Physical or digital location for subscription details
Other Online Accounts	
Account Name	Enter the name of the account/platform
Username/Email	Enter the username or email linked to the account
Password	Enter the password
Two-Factor Authentication	Enable/disable instructions to access
Backup Email/Phone	Enter backup email or phone number for recovery
Documents Location	Physical or digital location for account details

,My uncle passed away without a clear will, and it caused disputes and tension in the family. If only we had a system like Family CEO to keep wills and legal documents up-to-date, it would have avoided all the confusion and legal issues we faced."

- Suyash Singh, Bhilwara

Chapter 9: Wills, Trusts, and Legal Documents

"A WELL-DOCUMENTED WILL IS THE VOICE THAT SPEAKS FOR YOU WHEN YOU'RE NOT THERE TO GUIDE YOUR FAMILY."

Overview:

Having a well-documented and legally binding **will**, along with other legal documents such as trusts and powers of attorney, is essential to ensuring that your assets are distributed according to your wishes. A will provides clarity and prevents confusion or disputes among family members after your passing. Without a proper will, legal disputes can arise, leading to emotional stress, financial burdens, and delayed distribution of assets.

In addition to a will, documents like **trusts** allow you to safeguard the interests of minors or dependents, ensuring their financial needs are met. Powers of attorney designate trusted individuals to make financial or medical decisions on your behalf if you become incapacitated. Proper legal planning ensures that your family avoids long and costly probate processes, while also ensuring that assets like property, bank accounts, investments, and personal items are transferred to the right people seamlessly.

Without proper **legal documentation**, families may find themselves locked in court battles, dealing with expensive legal fees, and navigating complicated inheritance laws. This also includes the risk of unintended heirs benefiting from the estate, or assets being distributed in a way that goes against your wishes. Regularly updating your will and legal documents as life circumstances change is crucial to keeping them valid and relevant.

Real-Life Examples:

1. In the famous case of **Jimi Hendrix**, the legendary musician passed away without leaving a valid will. For over 30 years, his estate was the subject of legal disputes between his family members. The lack of a clear legal document outlining his wishes caused a lengthy and expensive court battle, which could have been avoided if Hendrix had documented his will properly. This case emphasizes the importance of having a valid and up-to-date will to avoid such disputes. Proper estate planning could

have spared his family the prolonged emotional and financial turmoil that followed.

2.   Also, a widely known case is the ongoing legal battle over the estate of the legendary musician **Prince**, who passed away in 2016 without leaving a will. His estate, valued at hundreds of millions of dollars, became the subject of numerous lawsuits involving potential heirs and the distribution of his assets. The absence of a clear will has led to prolonged legal disputes that have yet to be fully resolved, with significant delays in the distribution of his wealth. This case illustrates the critical importance of having a valid, up-to-date will in place, as it could have prevented such costly and emotionally draining conflicts.

Actionable Steps:

- Fill in the details for all your **wills**, **trusts**, and **legal documents**, ensuring each has a designated storage location and responsible contact.

- Update the template with recent changes to the will or trust and ensure beneficiaries are aware of their entitlements.

- Keep all legal documents, including powers of attorney and succession plans, accessible to trusted family members or legal advisors.

- Ensure any conditions tied to the distribution of assets or succession of businesses are clearly outlined.

Tip 1: Keep original copies of your will, trust agreements, and powers of attorney in a secure but accessible location.

Tip 2: Review and update legal documents every few years, or when major life changes occur (marriage, birth, death).

Tip 3: Clearly designate executors and trustees, and ensure they have a copy of relevant documents.

Wills, Trusts, & Legal Documents Tracker

Category	Details (Fill it with a blue or black pen)
Wills	
Will Created Date	Enter the date the will was created
Location of Original Will	Physical or digital storage location of the will
Executor Name	Enter the executor's full name
Executor Contact Information	Enter the executor's phone number and email
Legal Firm/Attorney Contact	List the contact information for the lawyer who handled the will
Beneficiaries	List the named will beneficiaries
Distribution of Assets	Brief description of how assets will be distributed
Date of Last Update	Enter the date of the most recent will update
Conditions of Will	Specify any conditions or special provisions
Trust Information	
Trust Name	Enter the name of the trust
Type of Trust	Enter the type of trust (Revocable, Irrevocable)
Trust Created Date	Enter the date the trust was created
Trustee Name	Enter the full name of the trustee
Trustee Contact Information	Enter the trustee's phone number and email
Beneficiaries of Trust	List the names of the trust beneficiaries
Trust Assets	List assets held in the trust (property, investments, etc.)
Trust Conditions	Specify any conditions tied to the trust's distribution
Location of Trust Documents	Physical or digital location of the trust documents
Date of Last Update	Enter the date of the most recent trust update

Power of Attorney (POA)	
POA Holder Name	Enter the full name of the person holding a POA
POA Contacts	Enter their phone number and email
Scope of Power	Enter the type of power granted (Financial, Medical, General)
POA Document Location	Physical or digital location of the POA document
Expiration Date (if any)	Enter the expiration date of the POA, if applicable
Succession Plan	
Business/Asset Name	Enter the name of the business or asset involved in the succession plan
Successor Name	Enter the full name of the successor
Successor Contact Information	Enter the successor's phone number and email
Transfer of Ownership Plan	Describe the process for transferring ownership of the asset or business
Legal Documents Location	Physical or digital location of succession documents
Conditions of Succession	Specify any conditions tied to the succession
Other Legal Documents	
Document Type	Enter type of document (e.g., Living Will, Health Directive)
Document Created Date	Enter the date the document was created
Document Location	Physical or digital location of the document
Contact Person	Enter the name of the person responsible for handling the document
Notes	Any special considerations or instructions regarding the document

Personal Notes

Chapter 10: Managing Employment Benefits and Retirement Plans

"DON'T LET YOUR HARD-EARNED RETIREMENT BENEFITS GET LOST! DOCUMENT THEM NOW TO PROTECT YOUR LOVED ONES, BECAUSE A WELL-ORGANIZED RECORD OF EMPLOYMENT BENEFITS IS THE BRIDGE THAT SUPPORTS YOUR FAMILY WHEN THEY NEED IT THE MOST."

Overview: Documenting employment benefits such as retirement plans, provident funds, gratuity, and employer-provided insurance is essential to ensure that your family can access these financial resources when needed. These benefits are often substantial and can provide critical financial support to your loved ones after your passing. However, without clear documentation or knowledge of how to claim these benefits, your family may face delays, confusion, and unnecessary stress.

Many employers offer valuable benefits that employees and their families are entitled to, including pension schemes, superannuation, group life insurance, and health benefits. If these benefits are not documented and communicated properly, family members may struggle to navigate the process of claiming them, especially during times of grief. It's important to keep track of all retirement accounts, employer-provided insurance policies, and any other benefits, along with instructions on how to access them.

By organizing employment benefit documents, detailing contacts within HR departments, and making your family aware of the processes involved, you ensure that these resources are readily available to your family, preventing financial hardships. Regularly updating this information is crucial, especially after job changes, promotions, or shifts in benefits.

Real-Life Examples:

1. A government employee in New Zealand passed away, and his widow struggled to claim his retirement benefits and employer-provided insurance because she didn't know where to start. The process of claiming the funds was slow, and she missed deadlines for some benefits. If her husband had clearly documented his retirement benefits, superannuation, and employer-provided insurance policies, she would have been able to claim them promptly and avoid unnecessary delays.

2.   Anjali's husband, Akash, had worked for a company that offered a generous provident fund and other retirement benefits. However, when Akash passed away suddenly, Anjali was left unsure of how to claim these funds. She didn't know who to contact at his workplace or what paperwork was needed. As a result, it took several months for her to figure out the process and access the money. If Akash had kept his employment benefits organized and informed his family about them, Anjali could have navigated the system smoothly and claimed the funds much more quickly, easing her financial stress during a difficult time.

Actionable Steps:

- Fill in all relevant details regarding your **employment benefits**, including salary, retirement plans, and employer-provided insurance.

- Keep digital copies of employment contracts, benefit plans, and retirement documents in a secure location.

- Ensure beneficiaries for retirement plans and insurance policies are up to date and properly documented.

- Regularly review and update this tracker to reflect changes in benefits or employer contributions.

This **Employment Benefits Tracker** helps ensure that all job-related information, including retirement benefits, salary, and insurance details, are organized and easily accessible.

Tip 1: Record details of retirement plans, including provident funds, pensions, and employer-sponsored benefits.

Tip 2: Note contact information for the benefits administrator or HR representative to ease claim processes.

Tip 3: Review benefit statements annually to make sure records are current.

Employment Benefits Tracker Template

Category	Details (Fill it with a blue or black pen)
Job Information	
Current Employer	Enter the name of your current employer
Position/Title	Enter your job title or position
Date of Employment Start	Enter the date you started with your employer
Employment Contract Location	Physical or digital location of the employment contract
Supervisor/Manager Contact	Enter the name, phone number, and email of your direct supervisor
HR Contact Information	Enter the contact details for the HR department
Salary & Compensation	
Annual Salary	Enter your current annual salary
Payment Frequency	[Monthly / Quarterly / Yearly]
Bonuses or Incentives	Enter details of any bonuses or incentives received
Payment Method	Enter how your salary is paid (bank transfer, cheque, etc.)
Retirement Benefits	
Retirement Plan Name	Enter the name of the retirement plan (e.g. Provident Fund, Pension)
Plan Provider	Enter the name of the financial institution or provider
Policy/Account Number	Enter the account or policy number
Current Balance	Enter the current balance in the retirement account
Employer Contribution	Enter the amount or percentage the employer contributes
Beneficiary Details	Enter the name of the designated plan beneficiary
Retirement Age	Enter the retirement age specified in the plan
Vesting Date (if applicable)	Enter the date when benefits are fully vested

Location of Retirement Documents	Physical or digital location of plan documents
Employer-Provided Insurance	
Insurance Type	(Life, Health, Disability)
Insurance Provider	Enter the name of the insurance company
Policy Number	Enter the policy number
Coverage Details	List coverage details (e.g., medical, dental, vision)
Start Date	Enter the start date of the insurance policy
Expiration Date	Enter the expiration date of the insurance policy
Monthly Premium	Enter the premium, if applicable
Employer Contribution	Enter the amount paid or the employer contribution
Beneficiary Details	Enter the name of the insurance policy beneficiary
Location of Insurance Documents	Physical or digital location of insurance documents
Gratuity/End-of-Service Benefits	
Gratuity Eligibility	Enter the eligibility conditions for gratuity
Gratuity Amount	Enter the current amount of gratuity benefits accrued
Gratuity Payment Method	Describe how the gratuity is paid (lump sum, installments, etc.)
Gratuity Documents Location	Physical or digital location of gratuity documents
Other Benefits	
Benefit Type	Enter the type of benefit (e.g., stock options, bonuses)
Provider	Enter the name of the benefit provider
Benefit Details	Enter details of the benefit (vesting period, options, etc.)
Documents Location	Physical or digital location of benefit documents

Personal Notes

Chapter 11: Managing Charity and Philanthropy

"YOUR GENEROSITY HAS SHAPED THE WORLD IN SMALL, BEAUTIFUL WAYS—MAKE SURE THOSE RIPPLES CONTINUE, EVEN AFTER YOU'RE GONE."

Overview: Philanthropy plays a significant role in the lives of many individuals, and it's essential to document charitable donations and philanthropic goals to ensure that these contributions continue after one's passing. Whether it's recurring donations to favorite causes or plans for larger, long-term giving, a clear record of your philanthropic efforts ensures that your values and legacy of giving are maintained.

Documenting your contributions helps family members understand which organizations are meaningful to you and allows them to continue your charitable work in alignment with your intentions. It's also important to specify any pledges or future commitments that you've made to nonprofits, NGOs, or charitable foundations. This ensures that your wishes are respected, and the organizations you supported can continue benefiting from your generosity. Without clear documentation, families might not be aware of your philanthropic goals, leading to interrupted support for the causes that matter most to you.

Real-Life Example:

In 2016, a philanthropist in South Africa passed away after a long life of making significant donations to various charities, including healthcare initiatives and education programs. However, after his death, his family struggled to identify which organizations he had supported and how he wanted to allocate his future donations. Because there was no clear record of his donation history or future philanthropic commitments, several charitable projects went unfunded, and his legacy of giving was not carried forward as he had intended. Had the philanthropist documented his charitable efforts and provided instructions for continuing them, his family could have honored his goals, and the charities he supported would not have been left in uncertainty.

Actionable Steps:

Document all **planned donations**, including the charity's name, amount, and payment schedule.

List all **philanthropy goals** and track progress towards meeting those goals, ensuring your charitable contributions align with your long-term vision.

Keep copies of **donation receipts** and related documents stored securely for future reference or tax purposes.

Update beneficiaries and ensure all **endowments** or **trusts** for charitable purposes are clearly defined and accessible.

Charity & Philanthropy Tracker

Category	Details (Fill it with a blue or black pen)
Planned Donations	
Charity/Organization Name	Enter the name of the charity or organization
Purpose of Donation	Enter the specific cause or event the donation supports
Donation Amount	Enter the planned donation amount
Donation Frequency	One-time, Monthly, Quarterly, Annually
Payment Method	Specify the payment method, bank transfer, cheque, etc.
Donation Date	Enter the date of the donation or next scheduled donation
Charity Contact Information	Enter the contact information for the charity or organization
Beneficiary/Donation Receipt Location	Physical or digital location of donation receipts
Philanthropy Goals	
Goal Name	Enter the name of the philanthropic goal or initiative
Goal Description	Provide a brief description of the goal
Target Amount	Enter the target amount for the philanthropy goal

Field	Description
Timeline	Enter the timeline for reaching the goal
Current Status	Track the progress toward reaching the goal
Beneficiary/End Recipient	Enter the name of the final recipient of the philanthropic donation
Contact Details of Beneficiary	Enter the contact details for the recipient or organization
Documents Location	Physical or digital location of related philanthropic documents
Endowments & Trusts for Charity	
Trust/Endowment Name	Enter the name of the endowment or trust set up for charity
Creation Date	Enter the date the trust/endowment was established
Trustee Name	Enter the name of the trustee overseeing the endowment
Trustee Contact	Enter the contact details of the trustee
Beneficiaries/Charities Covered	List the charities or organizations benefiting from the trust
Endowment Amount	Enter the initial amount of the endowment
Annual Disbursement Amount	Enter the amount disbursed annually to the charity
Trust/Endowment Documents Location	Physical or digital location of trust/endowment documents
Recurring Donations	
Charity Name	Enter the name of the charity
Recurring Donation Amount	Enter the recurring donation amount
Frequency of Donation	Specify the frequency (monthly, quarterly, etc.)
Next Payment Date	Enter the next scheduled payment date
Payment Method	Specify how the donation is made (bank transfer, standing order)
Contact Information	Enter the contact details of the charity
Documents Location	Physical or digital location of recurring donation records

Personal Notes

Tip 1: Document recurring donations, including the organization's name, donation amount, and frequency.

Tip 2: Record any pledges made to charitable causes and update the tracker once commitments are fulfilled.

Tip 3: Note tax benefits associated with donations to ensure proper documentation for tax deductions.

"We didn't know my father's wishes for his funeral, and making those decisions during our grief was incredibly difficult. We never realized how important it was to document even something as sensitive as funeral wishes. Family CEO would have helped us document his last wishes and spared us from making tough choices during such an emotional time."

- Deepak Agarwal, Ahmedabad

Chapter 12: Planning Funeral Arrangements and Last Wishes

"PLANNING YOUR FAREWELL TODAY IS AN ACT OF LOVE, SPARING YOUR FAMILY FROM UNCERTAINTY AND LETTING THEM FOCUS ON HONORING YOU."

Overview: Planning and documenting your funeral arrangements and last wishes is a thoughtful way to ease the burden on your family during an emotionally challenging time. By clearly outlining your preferences for last rites, the type of service you want, and any specific requests regarding burial or cremation, you prevent potential disputes and confusion among family members. Funeral preferences can vary greatly based on religious beliefs, cultural traditions, or personal values, making it important to document your wishes explicitly.

Without proper guidance, families are often left struggling to decide how to honor their loved ones, which can lead to disagreements or uncertainty. By planning in advance, you help your family focus on grieving and celebrating your life, rather than managing logistical challenges. It's also beneficial to outline details such as organ donation preferences, religious ceremonies, and any pre-arranged services, ensuring that everything is handled smoothly.

Real-Life Example: Funeral Arrangements

1)   Vijay's sudden passing left his family divided on how to conduct his funeral. While some family members wanted a traditional Hindu cremation, others suggested a modern memorial service to reflect his more progressive views. The lack of clear instructions led to tension and delays in planning the ceremony, causing further emotional distress. If Vijay had documented his funeral preferences, his family would have known exactly how he wanted to be honored, avoiding the internal conflict during such a sensitive time.

2)   In a well-known case from the UK, pop star **George Michael** passed away in 2016. Despite his global fame, Michael did not leave behind detailed funeral arrangements, leading to significant delays in organizing his service. His family faced confusion regarding his final wishes, and disagreements arose about how his funeral should be conducted. If Michael had left explicit instructions for his last rites and memorial, his

family could have avoided the uncertainty and provided him the tribute he wanted, without the prolonged emotional strain.

3)　　　In 2020, the author's father, **Dasharath Sonar**, a talented drawing artist and a deeply nature-loving individual, made it clear that he wished to forgo the traditional wood cremation in favor of electronic cremation. His motivation was to reduce harm to the environment by preventing the cutting down of trees. He also requested that pure ghee should not be used as part of the cremation process, as fuel for burning the wood, and that his ashes not be immersed in the River, Ganga, mindful of the pollution it could cause. Although these wishes were not formally documented, his clear communication allowed the family to honor his environmentally conscious values swiftly and without confusion, making the process both respectful and aligned with his love for nature.

Real-Life Example: Organ Donation

1) **Jerry Orbach**, a well-known actor from the TV series *Law & Order*, was a passionate advocate for organ donation. After his death in 2004, he became a cornea donor, giving the gift of sight to two individuals. His commitment to organ donation was well-documented, and his advocacy significantly raised awareness of the importance of organ and tissue donation. The legacy of his decision continues to influence many who choose to donate their organs to save lives.

2) In 1994, **Nicholas Green**, a 7-year-old boy from California, was tragically killed during a robbery while vacationing with his family in Italy. His parents made the decision to donate his organs, which saved the lives of seven Italians. The Green family's decision sparked widespread awareness about organ donation in Italy, leading to a significant increase in the number of donors across the country. To this day, Nicholas Green is remembered for his life-saving contributions.

3) Indian actress **Aishwarya Rai Bachchan**, one of the most recognized figures in Indian cinema, pledged to donate her eyes after her death to the Eye Bank Association of India. Her public declaration inspired many across India to consider eye and organ donation, promoting awareness about the need for organ donors and helping to destigmatize the practice. As a public figure, her choice brought significant visibility to the cause.

4) Reg Green, the father of Nicholas Green, became an outspoken advocate for organ donation after the loss of his son. Reg's advocacy efforts have encouraged thousands of families around the world to consider organ donation. He has authored books, given speeches, and been featured in documentaries, making a global impact on organ donation awareness.

Actionable Steps:

1.   Document your **last rites** preferences, including cultural or religious customs, burial or cremation wishes, and any pre-arranged plans.
2.   If you wish to be an **organ donor**, include details about registration and contact information for the medical facility.
3.   If you have **pre-paid funeral plans**, provide detailed information about the service provider and plan specifics.
4.   Ensure your family knows where to find **funeral documents,** including pre-paid plans and instructions for handling funeral expenses

Tip 1: Specify your preferred funeral arrangements, including burial or cremation preferences, and communicate them to a trusted person.

Tip 2: List contact information for any funeral service providers or religious organizations involved.

Tip 3: Update this tracker whenever there are changes to your wishes or arrangements.

Funeral Arrangements Tracker Template

Category	Details (Fill it with a blue or black pen)
Last Rites Preferences	
Religious or Cultural Rites	
Burial or Cremation	
Location of Burial/Cremation	
Memorial Service Location	
Special Instructions for Service	
Preferred Funeral Director/Company	
Contact Information	
Organ Donation	
Organ Donation Wishes	
Organs to Donate	
Registration Details	
Medical Facility Contact	
Organ Donation Documents Location	
Pre-Arranged Funeral Plans	
Funeral Service Provider	
Pre-Paid Plan Details	
Service Inclusions	

Funeral Plan Documentation	Physical or digital location of pre-paid plan documents
Contact Information	Provide the contact details of the funeral service provider
Special Requests	
Music or Readings	List any specific music or readings you would like at the funeral or memorial
Flowers or Donations in Lieu	Specify whether you prefer flowers or donations to a charity in your memory
Guest List	Optional: List important people you'd like to ensure are invited
Memorial Type	Describe the type of memorial (e.g., traditional, celebration of life) or leave it up to the family
Funeral Expenses & Payments	
Estimated Funeral Expenses	Enter estimated costs for the funeral
Source of Funds	Specify how funeral expenses will be covered (e.g., insurance, pre-paid plan, savings)
Contact for Funeral Expenses	Enter the name and contact information of the person responsible for handling payments
Funeral Documents Location	Physical or digital location of documents related to funeral expenses
Additional Preferences	
Funeral Dress Code	Enter any special requests for attire, such as traditional dress
Eulogies	Specify who you would like to give a eulogy or speech at the service
Special Rituals or Customs	List any family or cultural customs you would like included in the service
Ashes Handling (if cremation)	Specify how you want your ashes handled (e.g., kept in an urn, scattered at a specific location)
Other Last Wishes	Enter any other personal requests or instructions

Personal Notes

Chapter 13: Ensuring Pet Care in Your Absence

"YOUR PETS LOVE YOU UNCONDITIONALLY—MAKE SURE THEY'RE CARED FOR WITH THE SAME LOVE AND ATTENTION WHEN YOU'RE NOT AROUND."

Overview:

Pets are beloved members of the family, and just like people, they require care and attention, especially in the event of an owner's sudden passing. Ensuring that your pet's medical needs, dietary preferences, and preferred caregivers are documented can help provide continuity of care in your absence. Properly outlining this information prevents your family from being overwhelmed, especially during a difficult time, and ensures your pet continues to receive the love and care they deserve.

Your pet's health records, dietary restrictions, regular routines, and even favorite toys should be documented, along with contact details for their veterinarian. Additionally, identifying a trusted caregiver and discussing plans with them in advance can alleviate any uncertainty about the pet's future. This level of preparation allows your family to focus on their own healing, knowing that your pet is in safe hands.

Real-Life Example:

1) After Jaya's unexpected passing, her family faced difficulty in taking care of her dog, Simba. Jaya had always been very particular about Simba's diet, medical care, and daily routines, but she hadn't left any instructions or records behind. The family was unaware of Simba's special dietary needs or who his regular veterinarian was, causing confusion and stress. Jaya had deeply loved Simba, and if she had documented his care details, her family could have ensured Simba was properly looked after without any disruption to his well-being.

2) In 2020, a woman from the UK passed away, leaving behind her three cats, but no clear instructions for their care. Her family was uncertain about who would take responsibility for the pets or what their care needs were. Eventually, after much confusion, one of her neighbors, who had often looked after the cats in the past, agreed to take them in. Had the

woman documented her plans for the cats' care, the transition would have been much smoother and less stressful for the animals and her loved ones.

Actionable Steps:

- Document all important details about your pet, including vet information, feeding schedules, and medication.

- Store all pet-related **insurance** and **vaccination records** in a secure location.

- Ensure your **caregivers** have clear instructions, including emergency contacts and medical details.

- Regularly update information about appointments, medications, and insurance renewals.

This **Pet Care Tracker** helps ensure your family has all the details they need to care for your pet in your absence or during emergencies. Using **FamilyCEO.in**, you can securely store and manage this information, ensuring your pet's care is seamless and worry-free.

Tip 1: Document veterinary details, including vaccination records, dietary requirements, and emergency contacts.

Tip 2: Provide clear instructions on pet routines, including feeding, grooming, and exercise.

Tip 3: Name a designated caregiver for your pet, and share their contact information.

Pet Care Tracker Template

Category	Details (Fill it with a blue or black pen)
Pet Information	
Pet Name	
Type of Pet	
Breed (if applicable)	
Date of Birth	
Microchip Number (if applicable)	

Physical Description	Enter a brief description of what your pet looks like (e.g.)
Current Medications	List any current medications your pet is taking
Allergy Information	List any known allergies
Favorite Food/Brand	Specify the brand and type of food your pet prefers
Veterinary Information	
Primary Veterinarian Name	Enter the name of your pet's primary veterinarian
Veterinary Clinic Name	Enter the clinic name
Clinic Address	Enter the clinic's address
Veterinarian Contact Information	Enter the phone number and email of the vet
Last Check-Up Date	Enter the date of the last check-up
Next Appointment Date	Enter the date of the next scheduled appointment
Vaccination Records Location	Physical or digital location of vaccination records
Pet Insurance	
Insurance Provider Name	Enter the name of the pet insurance provider
Policy Number	Enter the policy number
Coverage Details	List the coverage details (e.g. veterinary care, accidents)
Monthly Premium	Enter the monthly premium
Policy Expiration Date	Enter the expiration date of the insurance policy
Insurance Documents Location	Physical or digital location of pet insurance documents
Caregivers & Emergency Contacts	
Primary Caregiver Name	Enter the name of the person who will care for your pet

Caregiver Contact Information	Enter the phone number and email of the caregiver
Caregiver Instructions	Provide specific instructions for the caregiver (feeding, walking, routine, etc.)
Backup Caregiver Name	Enter the name of the backup caregiver
Backup Caregiver Contact Info	Enter the contact details for the backup caregiver
Emergency Contact for Pet	Provide the name and contact of someone to contact in case of an emergency
Feeding & Routine Information	
Feeding Schedule	Enter your pet's daily feeding schedule
Favorite Treats	List the favorite treats or snacks your pet loves
Exercise/Walking Routine	Describe your pet's exercise or walking routine
Grooming Preferences	Specify your pet's grooming needs or preferences
Special Needs/Medical Instructions	
Special Medical Conditions	List any specific medical conditions your pet has
Medication & Dosage	List the medication and dosage
Medical Emergency Instructions	Provide specific instructions in case of a medical emergency
Documents Location	Physical or digital location of medical records
Boarding/Kennel Information	
Preferred Boarding/Kennel Name	Enter the name of the preferred boarding facility or kennel
Boarding/Kennel Contact Info	Enter the phone number and address
Special Instructions for Boarding	Enter specific instructions for boarding your pet

Personal Notes

,My father owned a small stationary supplying business, but when he passed, we had no idea how to manage the operations or what legal steps to take. If Family CEO had existed then, we could have avoided months of confusion and legal battles by having a clear business succession plan."

- Lovish Garg, Delhi

Chapter 14: Managing Business Ownership and Succession Planning

"PLANNING YOUR BUSINESS SUCCESSION TODAY MEANS GIVING YOUR FAMILY AND EMPLOYEES CONFIDENCE IN TIMES OF CHANGE."

Overview: For business owners, creating a clear succession plan and documenting ownership details are crucial steps to ensuring that your business continues to function smoothly in your absence. A well-prepared succession plan outlines who will take over the leadership, manage daily operations, and handle financial and legal matters. This not only provides stability for the business but also helps prevent costly legal disputes and financial difficulties for your family.

Without proper documentation, your family or business partners may be left scrambling to figure out how the business is structured, who holds key responsibilities, and how to manage assets. Succession planning also ensures that your business legacy continues, preserving the hard work you've put into building it. In some cases, a family member may be prepared to step in, while in others, external managers or partners may need to be involved. Proper planning alleviates uncertainty and makes the transition of ownership or leadership seamless.

Real-Life Example:

1. Rohit owned a small but successful manufacturing business that employed several people and contributed significantly to his family's income. However, when Rohit passed away unexpectedly, his family was left in a state of confusion. They didn't know who was responsible for day-to-day operations, how the finances were managed, or even the exact structure of the business. For months, the business struggled, and clients became uncertain, leading to lost contracts and financial strain. If Rohit had documented a clear business succession plan, his family could have taken control quickly and ensured the smooth continuation of the company, minimizing financial losses and uncertainty.

2. In 2019, a family in the U.S. inherited a family-owned restaurant after the death of its founder, but because there was no documented

succession plan, disagreements between the siblings led to the restaurant's closure. With no clear leadership, the business fell into disrepair, and eventually, they had to sell it at a loss. If the founder had put in place a plan for who would manage the restaurant, along with detailed business information, the business could have continued as a profitable venture for future generations.

3. In 2008, in a large housing colony where the author lived, a kind and generous businessman on the 4th floor was well-respected by all. During the Ganesha festival, he made a significant contribution to the society by funding the temple construction and donating the idol. Tragically, just two days later, he died in a road accident while returning from a ghat section. He left behind a wife and three young daughters who were completely unaware of his business affairs, which he managed with three partners. Initially, his partners expressed grief, but soon began avoiding compensating his family for his share of the business. As a chartered accountant, I stepped in to help, spending six months negotiating with his partners and sorting through his financials. We secured a fair settlement, along with addressing home loan liabilities and negotiating with the insurance and transport companies involved in the accident. This experience highlighted how crucial it is to document business details and have a succession plan to prevent leaving a family in financial and emotional distress.

Actionable Steps:

- Document all **business ownership** details, including ownership structure, financials, and key personnel roles.
- Outline your **succession plan**, ensuring your successor is well-prepared and trained to take over the business smoothly.
- Keep all **legal and financial documents** related to the business stored securely and easily accessible.
- Regularly review and update this template to reflect changes in business operations, finances, or succession plans.

This **Business Ownership & Succession Planning Tracker** ensures that your business continues to operate smoothly in your absence or during a transition of ownership. Using **FamilyCEO.in**, you can securely manage and store all important business details, making succession planning clear and accessible for your family or business partners.

Business Ownership & Succession Planning Tracker Template

Category	Details (Fill it with a blue or black pen)
Business Information	
Business Name	Enter the name of the business
Business Type	Enter the type of business (LLC, partnership, sole proprietorship, etc.)
Industry	Specify the industry (e.g., retail, technology, manufacturing)
Date of Business Establishment	Enter the date the business was established
Business Registration Number	Enter the business registration number
Tax Identification Number	Enter the business's tax identification number
Location of Business Documents	Physical or digital location of registration and tax documents
Business Address	Enter the main office address of the business
Business Contact Information	Enter the business phone number and email
Ownership Structure	
Ownership Percentage	Enter your ownership percentage in the business
Co-Owners/Partners	List any co-owners or partners and their ownership stakes
Partnership/Shareholder Agreements	Enter the location of partnership or shareholder agreements
Location of Ownership Documents	Physical or digital location of ownership documents
Key Business Financials	
Business Bank Accounts	List the business's bank account details, including account number and balance
Business Loans or Liabilities	List any outstanding loans or liabilities associated with the business

Monthly Revenue	Enter the current average monthly revenue
Annual Revenue	Enter the annual revenue/income
Profit Margin	Enter the average profit margin
Business Valuation	Enter the most recent valuation of the business
Financial Documents Location	Physical or digital location of financial statements, tax filings, and other documents
Key Personnel & Roles	
Key Manager(s)	Enter the names and roles of key managers or executives
Successor for Key Roles	List successors in case of a change or transition
Contact Information for Key Personnel	Enter the contact details for key managers or executives
Roles & Responsibilities	Describe the key roles and responsibilities for daily business operations
Key Vendor/Client Contracts	List the main vendors and clients, including contract details and terms for each one
Location of Contracts	The online or physical location of vendor/client contracts
Business Insurance	
Insurance Provider Name	Enter the name of the business insurance provider
Insurance Policy Number	Enter the insurance policy number
Coverage Details	List coverage details (e.g., property, liability, employee insurance)
Insurance Expiration Date	Enter the expiration date of the policy
Monthly Premium	Enter the monthly premium
Insurance Documents Location	Physical or digital location of insurance policy documents

Succession Planning	
Successor Name	Enter the name of the person who will take over the business.
Successor Contact Information	Enter the successor's phone number and email.
Training Plan for Successor	Describe the training plan for the successor to ensure a smooth transition.
Transfer of Ownership Plan	Specify how ownership will be transferred (e.g., sale, gift, inheritance).
Legal Documents for Transfer	Physical or digital location of legal documents related to the ownership transfer.
Power of Attorney (if applicable)	Enter the name of the person holding POA for business decisions.
Legal Advisor/Attorney Contact	Enter the name and contact details of the business's legal advisor or attorney.
Additional Instructions	Provide any additional instructions or details related to the business transition.
Contingency Planning	
Backup Successor Name	Enter the name of a backup successor in case the primary successor is unable to assume the role.
Contingency Plan for Key Events	List key events or risks that may require immediate action (e.g., financial downturn, legal disputes).
Emergency Contact Information	Provide emergency contact information for key personnel during the transition.
Legal Documents for Contingencies	Physical or digital location of legal documents related to contingency planning.

Personal Notes

Tip 1: Keep business ownership documents, partnership agreements, and shareholder details in a secure place.

Tip 2: Outline a clear succession plan, specifying who will take over in your absence.

Tip 3: Review business succession plans periodically to ensure they remain up-to-date.

Chapter 15: Securing Permissions and Access to Important Information

"GIVING TRUSTED INDIVIDUALS THE RIGHT PERMISSIONS TODAY ENSURES THAT YOUR FAMILY CAN MANAGE CRUCIAL RESPONSIBILITIES WITHOUT UNNECESSARY OBSTACLES."

Overview: Granting trusted individuals access to important financial accounts, safes, or legal documents is crucial in ensuring that your assets and affairs can be managed smoothly in your absence. This access should be carefully documented and managed to protect against unauthorized use while ensuring that, when the time comes, the right people can step in without unnecessary delays. Establishing secure protocols, such as using two-factor authentication or trusted access tools, helps safeguard your valuable assets while still allowing quick and easy access for those responsible.

Without proper documentation of access permissions, families can face logistical barriers during already difficult times, like not being able to access bank accounts, important legal papers, or safety deposit boxes. By organizing and securing this information, you make it easy for your family to handle urgent matters promptly, avoiding financial and legal setbacks.

Real-Life Example:

1. Priya knew her husband kept important documents, including property deeds and investment records, in a home safe. However, after his sudden passing, she realized she didn't have the combination to access the safe. It took her several days to get a locksmith, delaying important decisions that required those documents. Had Priya's husband shared the safe's combination in a secure way beforehand, such as documenting it in an encrypted file or trusted legal repository, the process would have been much simpler and faster for her during a difficult time.

2. In 2018, a family in Australia struggled after the sudden death of their father, who had several bank accounts and safes, but no one had the access codes or login credentials. The family had to go through a lengthy process of resetting passwords and retrieving access, causing

stress and delays. A simple security tracker with permissions and access details would have allowed the family to settle accounts faster and with less hassle.

Actionable Steps:

- Document all **access permissions** for family members, trusted advisors, business partners, and any others who have access to your accounts or assets.
- Specify **security protocols**, such as two-factor authentication (2FA), and ensure that necessary credentials are shared securely.
- Maintain a clear **emergency access plan** for family members or designated contacts to manage your assets or accounts in case of unforeseen circumstances.
  Regularly review and update security permissions, access codes, and passwords to ensure security.

Security & Permissions Tracker

Category	Details (Fill it with a blue or black pen)
Access Permissions for Family Members	
Family Member Name	Enter the name of the family member (e.g., ...)
Relationship	Indicate their relationship to you (e.g., spouse, child, etc.)
Access Level	Specify what they can access: financial accounts, real estate, digital assets, etc.
Permissions Start Date	Enter the date when access starts
Permissions End Date (if applicable)	Enter the date when access expires, if temporary
Security Credentials Shared	Specify if passwords, PINs, or other security credentials are shared
Two-Factor Authentication (2FA) Status	Enter if 2FA is enabled and how to access it
Emergency Contact Role	Specify if this family member is a designated emergency contact
Documents Location	Physical or digital location of documents regarding permissions

Trusted Advisors & Professional Access	
Advisor Name	Enter the name of the trusted advisor (financial, legal, etc.)
Role/Title	Specify their role (financial advisor, attorney, etc.)
Access Level	Specify what they can access (bank accounts, legal documents, etc.)
Permissions Start Date	Enter the date when access starts
Permissions End Date (if applicable)	Enter the date when access expires
Security Credentials Shared	Specify what credentials are shared (passwords, keys, etc.)
Two-Factor Authentication (2FA) Status	Enter if 2FA is enabled and how to access it
Documents Location	Physical or digital location of permissions documents
Business Partners Access	
Partner Name	Enter the name of the business partner
Business Role	Specify their role in the business (co-owner, partner, etc.)
Access Level	Specify what they can access (business bank accounts, contracts, etc.)
Permissions Start Date	Enter the date when access starts
Permissions End Date (if applicable)	Enter the date when access expires
Security Credentials Shared	Specify what credentials are shared (passwords, keys, etc.)
Two-Factor Authentication Status	Enter if 2FA is enabled and how to access it
Business Documents Location	Physical or digital location of permissions documents
Digital Security Protocols	
Account Name	Enter the name of the digital account (email, cloud storage, etc.)

Username/Email Associated	Enter the username or email associated with the account
Password	Enter the password for the account
Two-Factor Authentication (2FA) Enabled	List 2FA and instructions to access 2FA
Backup Method for 2FA	Enter the backup recovery options (email, phone, etc.)
Password Manager Used	Note if a password manager was used and how to access it
Security Questions & Answers	List security questions and answers for account recovery
Location of Security Credentials	Physical or digital location of credentials
Physical Security & Safe Access	
Safe or Lockbox Location	Enter the physical location of any safe or lockbox
Safe Access Code/Key	List the access code or key location for the safe
Permissions to Access Safe	List family members or advisors who can access the safe
Emergency Access Protocol	Specify emergency protocols for safe access
Security Documents Location	Physical or digital location of security documents
Emergency Access Protocols	
Emergency Contact Name	Enter the name of the emergency contact who will have full access in case of emergency
Contact Information	Enter the phone number and email for the emergency contact
Emergency Plan Location	Physical or digital location of emergency plan documents
Instructions for Emergency Access	Enter specific instructions for accessing critical accounts or assets in an emergency

Personal Notes

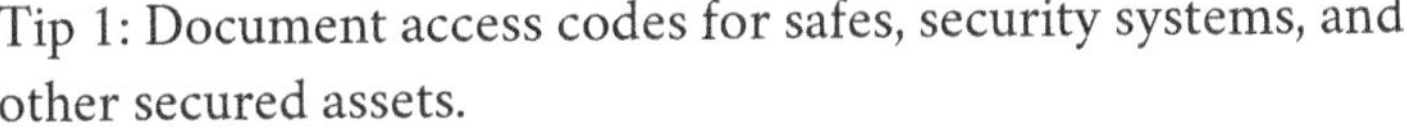

Tip 1: Document access codes for safes, security systems, and other secured assets.

Tip 2: Clearly designate which trusted individuals have access to sensitive information.

Tip 3: Periodically review and update permissions to ensure that access remains appropriate.

Chapter 16: Managing Nominations for Financial Accounts

"HAVING YOUR NOMINEES CLEARLY DOCUMENTED ENSURES THAT YOUR HARD-EARNED ASSETS ARE TRANSFERRED SMOOTHLY, PROVIDING SECURITY AND STABILITY TO YOUR LOVED ONES."

Overview:

Documenting and regularly updating nominees for your bank accounts, insurance policies, and investments is essential to ensure a smooth transfer of funds to the intended beneficiary after your passing. This avoids legal complications, disputes, and delays in transferring assets to the rightful person. Regularly reviewing and updating nominations, especially after major life events such as marriage, divorce, or the birth of a child, ensures that your wishes are fulfilled without confusion.

Real-Life Example:

In a widely publicized case in India, a man passed away without updating the nominees for his life insurance policy and bank accounts. The policy still listed his late father as the nominee, which led to a legal battle between his surviving family members. Since the insurance company refused to release the funds until the legal issues were resolved, it caused significant delays and emotional distress. This situation could have been easily avoided if the man had regularly updated his nomination forms to reflect his current family situation.

Actionable Steps:

1. Document all **nominees** for your bank accounts, investments, insurance policies, and real estate, ensuring that these details are up to date.
2. Store **nomination forms** securely and make sure the **nominees' contact information** is easily accessible.
3. Regularly review and update **nomination details** to reflect any life changes or new beneficiaries.
4. Ensure all legal nomination documents are properly filed and accessible to trusted family members or legal advisors.

Nominations Management Tracker

Category	Details (Fill it with a blue or black pen)
Bank Accounts	
Bank Name	
Account Number	
Nominee Name	
Relationship to Account Holder	
Nomination Date	
Beneficiary Contact Information	
Location of Nomination Documents	
Fixed Deposits & Investments	
Investment Type	
Investment Provider Name	
Account/Policy Number	
Nominee Name	
Relationship to Account Holder	
Nomination Date	
Beneficiary Contact Information	
Location of Nomination Documents	
Insurance Policies	
Insurance Provider Name	
Policy Number	
Type of Insurance	
Nominee Name	

Relationship to Policy Holder	Enter the relationship to the policy holder
Nomination Date	Enter the date when the nominee was added
Beneficiary Contact Information	Enter the phone number/email of the nominee
Location of Insurance Documents	Physical or digital location of policy documents

Retirement/Pension Plans

Pension/Retirement Plan Name	Enter the name of the retirement plan
Account Number/Plan ID	Enter the account or plan number
Nominee Name	Enter the name of the nominee
Relationship to Account Holder	Enter the relationship to the account holder
Nomination Date	Enter the date when the nominee was added
Beneficiary Contact Information	Enter the phone number/email of the nominee
Location of Nomination Documents	Physical or digital location of nomination documents

Real Estate Properties

Property Address	Enter the full address of the property
Ownership Type	Joint, Sole Ownership, etc.
Nominee Name	Enter the name of the nominee
Relationship to Property Owner	Enter the relationship to the property owner
Nomination Date	Enter the date when the nominee was added
Beneficiary Contact Information	Enter the phone number/email of the nominee
Location of Ownership/Nomination Documents	Physical or digital location of ownership/nomination documents

Other Assets & Accounts	
Asset Type	Enter the type of asset (e.g. vehicle, jewelry...)
Nominee Name	Enter the name of the nominee
Relationship to Asset Owner	Enter the relationship to the asset owner
Nomination Date	Enter the date when the nominee was added
Beneficiary Contact Information	Enter the phone number/email of the nominee
Location of Nomination Documents	Physical or digital location of nomination form

Tip 1: Regularly update nominee details for all accounts, policies, and investments to reflect current circumstances.

Tip 2: Make sure each nominee knows what they have been nominated for and where the relevant documents are kept.

Tip 3: Verify that nominee records match with account or policy documents.

Personal Notes

Chapter 17: Trusts for Dependents or Minors

"SETTING UP A TRUST TODAY SECURES YOUR LOVED ONES' FUTURE, ENSURING THEIR NEEDS ARE MET AND YOUR WISHES ARE HONORED WITHOUT COMPLICATIONS."

Overview: Establishing trusts for minors or dependents provides long-term financial security, ensuring their needs are met in your absence. Documenting the trust and including clear instructions about how the funds will be managed, who the trustee is, and how to contact them, ensures that the transition is seamless. Trusts are particularly important for families with young children or dependents who may not be able to manage their finances independently.

Real-Life Example:

1. In 2015, a wealthy family in Singapore set up a trust for their minor children to secure their financial future. However, when the father passed away suddenly, the family was unable to reach the trustee, and there were no clear instructions on how the funds were to be accessed. As a result, the children's financial needs went unmet for several months, causing unnecessary hardship. This delay could have been avoided if the trust had been properly documented with clear contact information and instructions for accessing funds.

2. When **Princess Diana** tragically passed away in 1997, she left behind a carefully structured trust for her two sons, **Prince William** and **Prince Harry**. The trust ensured that the inheritance from their mother was protected until they reached a certain age and maturity to handle the funds responsibly. Diana had clear instructions on how the trust should be managed, providing for her sons' financial security and future needs. By establishing this trust, Diana ensured that her sons were financially cared for without relying on third parties or risking any mismanagement of their inheritance.

3. **John Paul Getty**, one of the richest men in the world, established trusts for his grandchildren and other family members to ensure their long-term financial security. His trusts were set up with specific instructions about

how the funds were to be managed, particularly because some beneficiaries were minors or lacked the financial expertise to manage such wealth. This foresight allowed his descendants to access funds for their education and other needs without overwhelming them with large inheritances at a young age. The trust provided stability and financial security while preventing the potential financial mismanagement that can occur when minors inherit vast sums of money.

Actionable Steps:

- Document all details of the **trust**, including its purpose, type, and agreement location.
- Ensure **trustee information** is up-to-date, with backup trustees named in case the primary trustee cannot fulfill their duties.
- Keep clear records of **beneficiaries**, their conditions for receiving trust benefits, and the schedule of distributions.
- Track **trust assets**, including their value, income generation, and management instructions, ensuring asset-related documents are stored securely.
- Maintain records of **disbursements** and ensure all **tax and legal** obligations for the trust are met, with trusted professionals involved.

Trusts Management Tracker Template (Trusts & Trustee Information)

Category	Details (Fill it with a blue or black pen)
Trust Name	Enter the name of the trust
Trust Type	(Revocable, Irrevocable, Charitable, etc.)
Date Established	Enter the date the trust was established
Purpose of the Trust	Briefly describe the purpose (e.g., education, healthcare, tax deductions)
Trust Agreement Location	Physical or digital location of the trust agreement documents
Trust Registration Number	Enter the registration number (if any), if applicable
Trustee Information	
Trustee Name	Enter the name of the trustee managing the trust

Trustee Contact Information	Enter the trustee's phone number, email, and address
Relationship to Beneficiaries	Enter the trustee's relationship to the trust beneficiaries
Trustee's Role & Responsibilities	Outline the trustee's key responsibilities
Trustee Appointment Date	Enter the date when the trustee was appointed
Location of Trustee Documents	Physical or digital location of trustee-related documents
Backup Trustee Name (if applicable)	Enter the name of the backup trustee
Backup Trustee Contact Information	Enter the phone number and email of the backup trustee
Beneficiary Information	
Beneficiary Name(s)	Enter the names of all beneficiaries (children, dependents, etc.)
Relationship to Trust Creator	Enter the relationship to the person who created the trust
Age of Beneficiaries	Enter the age of each beneficiary
Conditions for Beneficiaries	List any conditions for receiving benefits (e.g., age, education)
Distribution Schedule	Specify when and how the trust benefits will be distributed (e.g., lump sum, annually)
Documents Location	Physical or digital location of beneficiary documents
Trust Assets	
Asset Type	Enter the type of asset held in the trust (e.g., real estate, cash, stocks)
Asset Value	Enter the current value of the asset
Asset Location	Physical or digital location of asset-related documents
Income Generated by Assets	Specify any income generated by trust assets (e.g., rental income, dividends)

Field	Description
Asset Management Instructions	Provide instructions for how the assets should be managed (e.g., reinvest, hold, sell)
Location of Asset Documents	Physical or digital location of asset documents
Trust Disbursement Information	
Disbursement Frequency	Enter how often disbursements are made (monthly, quarterly, annually)
Disbursement Amount	Enter the amount of each disbursement
Conditions for Disbursement	Specify any conditions for release (e.g., age, educational completion, age)
Payment Method for Beneficiaries	Specify the payment method (bank transfer, cheque, etc.)
Location of Disbursement Records	Physical or digital location of disbursement records
Tax & Legal Considerations	
Tax ID Number for Trust	Enter the tax identification number for the trust, if applicable
Tax Advisor Name	Enter the name of the tax advisor managing trust-related tax
Tax Advisor Contact Information	Enter the phone number and email of the tax advisor
Trust Tax Filing Date	Enter the [illegible]
Legal Advisor Name	Enter the name of financial/legal advisor managing the trust
Legal Advisor Contact Information	Enter the phone number and email of the legal advisor
Legal Documents Location	Physical or digital location of tax and legal documents

Tip 1: Document the trust agreement, including trustee information and terms of the trust.

Tip 2: Outline any conditions or milestones for accessing funds (e.g., reaching a certain age).

Tip 3: Review the trust annually to ensure it aligns with the current needs of the beneficiaries.

Personal Notes

Chapter 18: Handling Tax and Legal Matters Efficiently

Overview: Keeping tax filings and legal matters in order helps your family avoid penalties, legal disputes, and unnecessary delays. Ensuring that tax returns, property taxes, and legal issues are up to date can save time and stress.

Real-Life Example:

1. In 2018, **Aretha Franklin**, the legendary singer, passed away without a will, leaving behind an estate worth million. Due to the lack of estate planning, her family was entangled in legal disputes over her assets, and tax issues surfaced. Unpaid taxes accumulated, leading to a lengthy court battle that could have been avoided with proper planning. Had she documented her tax obligations and created a clear legal will, her family would have been spared years of stress and financial burden.

2. In 2016, the musician **Prince** passed away without a will, leaving an estate valued at an estimated $300 million. The lack of proper estate planning resulted in a complex and lengthy legal battle over his assets, including unresolved property tax and estate tax issues. With no will or tax planning documents, Prince's estate faced substantial estate taxes, reportedly reaching up to 50% of his estate's value, which had to be paid to the U.S. federal government and the state of Minnesota. The lack of planning not only delayed the distribution of his assets to his heirs but also caused financial stress due to the large tax burden that could have been mitigated with proper tax and legal arrangements. Had Prince structured his estate with tax planning and documented legal matters in order, his heirs would have been spared the complications of unpaid taxes and legal battles, ensuring a smoother transition of wealth.

Actionable Steps:
1. Document all **tax-related** information, including past filings, pending liabilities, and refund statuses, ensuring that key dates and amounts are tracked.
2. Maintain a clear record of your **legal advisors** and **legal documents** (wills, POAs, contracts), with all relevant contact information.
3. Keep all **tax filings** and **legal documents** organized in a secure location and easily accessible to your family or trusted contacts.
4. Regularly update tax and legal records to ensure compliance and track important deadlines, particularly for tax filings and property taxes.

Tax and Legal Matters Tracker Template

Category	Details (Fill it with a blue or black pen)
Tax Filing Information	
Taxpayer Identification Number (TIN/PAN)	Enter your TIN or PAN number
Tax Filing Status	Enter your current tax filing status (Filed, Pending)
Last Tax Filing Date	Enter the date of the most recent tax filing
Tax Year	Enter the applicable tax year
Tax Advisor/Accountant Name	Enter the name of your tax advisor or accountant
Tax Advisor Contact Information	Enter phone number and email of the tax advisor
Documents Location	Physical or digital location of tax returns, documents, and receipts
Refund Status	Enter the status of any tax refund, if applicable
Next Filing Deadline	Enter the due date for the next tax filing
Pending Tax Liabilities	
Tax Type	Income tax, Property tax, GST, etc.
Tax Year	Enter the applicable tax year
Outstanding Amount	Enter the amount of pending taxes

Payment Due Date	Enter the payment due date
Payment Method	Specify how the payment will be made (bank transfer, cheque, etc.)
Late Payment Penalties	Enter any applicable late payment penalties or interest
Tax Liability Documents Location	Physical or digital location of tax liability documents

Property Tax Information

Property Address	Enter the address of the property
Annual Property Tax Amount	Enter the amount of property tax due annually
Payment Due Date	Enter the due date for property tax payments
Payment Method	Specify how the payment will be made (bank transfer, cheque, etc.)
Tax Documents Location	Physical or digital location of property tax documents

Legal Advisor Information

Legal Advisor Name	Enter the name of your legal advisor or lawyer
Legal Advisor Firm	Enter the name of the law firm
Legal Advisor Contact Information	Enter the phone number and email of the legal advisor
Legal Representation Areas	Specify the areas the legal advisor handles (e.g., estate planning, business law)
Last Contact Date	Enter the date of the last consultation with the legal advisor
Documents Location	Physical or digital location of legal documents

Legal Documents

| Will & Testament | Enter the location of the will and any updates made |
| Power of Attorney (POA) | Enter the details of any power of attorney |

Trust Deeds	Enter the details and location of any trust deeds
Real Estate Titles	Enter the location of property titles and deeds
Legal Contracts & Agreements	Specify the type of contracts (business, rental agreement, etc.)
Legal Document Location	Physical or digital location of all legal documents
Business Tax Information	
Business Name	Enter the name of the business
Business Registration Number	Enter the business's registration number
GST/VAT Identification Number	Enter the GST or VAT registration number
Last Business Tax Filing Date	Enter the date of the most recent business tax filing
Business Tax Advisor Name	Enter the name of the business tax advisor
Business Tax Advisor Contact Information	Enter the phone number and email of the advisor
Business Tax Documents Location	Physical or digital location of business tax filings
Other Legal Matters	
Ongoing Legal Disputes	Specify any ongoing legal disputes and their status
Court Dates	Enter upcoming court dates, if applicable
Opposing Party & Legal Representation	Enter the names of opposing parties and their legal representatives
Documents Location	Physical or digital location of dispute-related documents

Tip 1: Keep copies of the last three years of tax returns, receipts, and any correspondence with tax authorities.

Tip 2: Maintain a record of property tax receipts and legal disputes (if any).

Tip 3: Update tax records and legal documents annually.

Chapter 19: Establishing Emergency Contacts for Family Assistance

HAVING A LIST OF TRUSTED EMERGENCY CONTACTS CAN BE THE DIFFERENCE BETWEEN CHAOS AND COMFORT FOR YOUR FAMILY DURING CRITICAL TIMES.

Overview: Having a clear list of emergency contacts, including family members, doctors, legal advisors, and other trusted individuals, ensures that your loved ones know exactly who to reach out to when facing unexpected events. Whether it's a medical emergency, a legal matter, or any situation requiring immediate attention, having this information readily available helps avoid confusion and ensures swift action during a critical time. This list should be easily accessible, covering everyone who might need to be contacted in the event of illness, injury, or death.

Real-Life Example:

In 2013, Paul Walker, the famous actor from the Fast & Furious franchise, tragically died in a car crash. After his passing, there was initial confusion about who was authorized to handle his legal and financial affairs. The absence of a clearly documented emergency contact list led to delays in decision-making, which ultimately prolonged the process of settling his estate and making necessary arrangements. This period of uncertainty added unnecessary stress to an already devastating situation for his family and close friends.

If an emergency contact list had been easily accessible, outlining the individuals to notify and their specific roles, many of these delays could have been avoided. His family could have acted more quickly and with greater confidence, ensuring that his legal and financial matters were handled efficiently. A well-prepared list of emergency contacts not only provides peace of mind but also prevents additional challenges during what is often an already emotionally overwhelming time.

Actionable Steps:

- Identify and document **primary** and **secondary emergency contacts**, ensuring their contact information is up-to-date.

- Assign clear **responsibilities** for each contact (e.g., manage finances, handle legal matters, oversee healthcare).
- Maintain a secure record of **healthcare providers**, including your primary doctor, clinic information, and health insurance details.
- Keep contact information for **financial** and **legal advisors** readily available and accessible to your family.
- Regularly review and update contact details and responsibilities, ensuring all key people are prepared in case of an emergency.

Emergency Contacts Tracker Template

Category	Details (Fill it with a blue or black pen)
Primary Emergency Contact	
Name	Enter the name of the primary emergency contact
Relationship	Enter the relationship to you (spouse, sibling, friend, etc.)
Phone Number	Enter the contact's primary phone number
Alternate Phone Number	Enter the contact's secondary phone number
Email Address	Enter the contact's email address
Home Address	Enter the contact's home address
Responsibilities	List the responsibilities this contact will have in an emergency (e.g., manage financials, oversee healthcare)
Documents Location	Physical or digital location of legal documents or instructions for this contact
Secondary Emergency Contact	
Name	Enter the name of secondary emergency contact
Relationship	Enter the relationship to you
Phone Number	Enter the contact's primary phone number
Alternate Phone	Enter the contact's secondary phone number
Email Address	Enter the contact's email address
Home Address	Enter the contact's home address
Responsibilities	List responsibilities of this contact

Documents Location	Physical or digital location of legal documents or instructions for this contact
Healthcare Provider Contact	
Primary Doctor Name	Enter the name of your primary doctor or healthcare provider
Clinic/Hospital	Enter the name of the clinic or hospital
Clinic/Hospital	Enter the address of the clinic or hospital
Doctor's Phone	Enter the doctor's phone number
Alternate Contact (if applicable)	Enter an alternate contact at the clinic or hospital
Medical Insurance	Enter the name of your health insurance provider
Policy Number	Enter your health insurance policy number
Documents Location	Physical or digital location of medical and insurance documents
Financial Advisor	
Name	Enter the name of your financial advisor
Firm Name	Enter the name of the advisory firm
Phone Number	Enter the contact's primary phone number
Email Address	Enter the contact's email address
Responsibilities	List financial responsibilities (e.g., manage investments, settle assets)
Documents Location	Physical or digital location of financial documents
Legal Advisor	
Name	Enter the name of your legal advisor
Law Firm Name	Enter the name of the law firm
Phone Number	Enter the contact's primary phone number
Email Address	Enter the contact's email address
Responsibilities	List legal responsibilities (e.g., execute will, handle succession)
Documents Location	Physical or digital location of legal documents
Other Key Contacts	
Contact Name	Enter the name of any other important emergency contact
Relationship	Enter the relationship (e.g., family friend, guardian)

Phone Number	List their emergency contact phone
Responsibilities	Describe specific responsibilities for this contact
Documents Location	Provide the location of related documents

Personal Notes

Tip 1: List primary and secondary emergency contacts, including family doctors, lawyers, and close friends.

Tip 2: Share this list with a trusted family member who may need to make quick decisions during emergencies.

Tip 3: Update contact details regularly to ensure accuracy.

Chapter 20: Preserving Your Family Legacy with a Family Tree

"UNDERSTANDING WHERE YOU COME FROM IS A GIFT TO FUTURE GENERATIONS—DOCUMENT YOUR FAMILY'S HISTORY SO THAT YOUR LEGACY LIVES ON."

Overview:

Documenting your family's lineage, key milestones, and personal history—known as **Vanshavali**—is a meaningful way to ensure that future generations remain connected to their roots. A **family tree** allows you to record and preserve the stories, traditions, and legacies of your ancestors, providing a sense of identity and continuity for your descendants. It's more than just a record of names and dates—it's a way to preserve the values, struggles, and achievements of past generations, allowing future ones to appreciate their heritage.

Having a documented Vanshavali ensures that crucial information about the family's background isn't lost over time, especially as older generations pass away. A well-maintained family tree can also serve as an essential tool for passing down property, heirlooms, or even legal claims. In many cultures, knowing your lineage is important for settling inheritance matters, property rights, and understanding familial responsibilities. By preserving this information, you help future generations stay connected to their identity and history, ensuring that the legacy of your family lives on perpetually.

Real-Life Example:

1. The **British Royal Family** is one of the most well-documented family trees in the world, tracing back thousands of years. The lineage of the royals is carefully maintained not only to preserve the historical significance but also to ensure the proper succession of titles, estates, and responsibilities. This documented family history has played a key role in maintaining the legacy and traditions of the monarchy over generations. The family tree is also a crucial reference for historians, scholars, and future generations of royals, ensuring continuity and connection with their heritage.

2. The **Kennedy family**, one of the most prominent political families in the U.S., has a meticulously maintained family tree, documenting its lineage and heritage. The Kennedy family tree not only chronicles the political and social achievements of its members but also preserves its deep Irish-American roots. This documentation helped later generations of Kennedys, such as Congressman Joseph Kennedy III, connect to their ancestors and understand the family's legacy in American politics and society. The family tree continues to be a source of pride and an important reminder of the family's influence and heritage.

3. In the 1970s, author **Alex Haley** traced his ancestry back through generations, documenting the lineage of his family in the famous book *Roots: The Saga of an American Family*. Haley's research and dedication to uncovering his family's history, which began in West Africa and led through the tragic period of slavery in America, brought the importance of family heritage and ancestry to the forefront for many African Americans. The story of Haley's family inspired countless people around the world to explore and document their own family trees, and *Roots* became a seminal work in understanding the impact of lineage on identity.

Actionable Steps:

- Include as much information as possible for **earlier generations** such as grandparents and great-grandparents, even if only partial information is available.
- Track and document **family origins** and **historical events** associated with the family, ensuring that future generations can trace the lineage.
- Keep all **family documents**—birth certificates, marriage licenses, and historical records—in an easily accessible location, either physically or digitally.
- Regularly update the family tree with new births, marriages, and other milestones, and encourage family members to contribute information about earlier generations

Family Tree Tracker Template

Category	Details (Fill it with a blue or black pen)
Head of Family (Current Generation)	
Name	Enter the full name of the family head
Date of Birth	Enter the date of birth
Date of Death (if applicable)	Enter the date of death
Spouse Name	Enter the spouse's name
Date of Birth	Enter spouse's date of birth
Date of Death (if applicable)	Enter the spouse's date of death
Marriage Date	Enter the date of marriage
Documents Location	Physical or digital location of marriage certificates, birth certificates, etc.
Children (Next Generation)	
Child Name	Enter the full name of the child
Date of Birth	Enter the child's date of birth
Date of Death (if applicable)	Enter the date of death
Spouse Name (if applicable)	Enter the child's spouse's name, if applicable
Child's Marriage Date (if applicable)	Enter the marriage date of the child
Child's Children Names	List the names of the child's children
Documents Location	Physical or digital location of birth certificates, marriage certificates, etc.
Grandchildren (Current)	
Grandchild Name	Enter the full name of the grandchild
Date of Birth	Enter the grandchild's date of birth
Parent Name	List the name of the parent to the child
Spouse Name (if applicable)	Enter the grandchild's spouse's name, if applicable
Grandchild's Marriage Date (if applicable)	Enter the grandchild's marriage date
Documents Location	Physical or digital location of birth certificates, marriage certificates, etc.

Extended Family (Siblings, Cousins, etc.)	
Sibling/Cousin Name	Enter the full name of your sibling or cousin
Date of Birth	Enter their date of birth
Date of Death (if applicable)	Enter the date of death
Spouse Name (if applicable)	Enter the spouse's name
Children's Names	Enter the names of their children
Documents Location	Please list the location of your relevant documents
Parents (Previous Generation)	
Father's Name	Enter your father's name
Father's Date of Birth	Enter your father's date of birth
Father's Date of Death (if applicable)	Enter his date of death
Mother's Name	Enter your mother's name
Mother's Date of Birth	Enter your mother's date of birth
Mother's Date of Death (if applicable)	Enter the date of death
Parents' Marriage Date	Enter the date of their marriage
Documents Location	Please list original location documents, birth, marriage certificates
Grandparents (Earlier Generation)	
Paternal Grandfather's Name	Enter your paternal grandfather's name
Paternal Grandfather's Date of Birth	Enter his date of birth
Paternal Grandfather's Date of Death (if applicable)	Enter the date of death
Paternal Grandmother's Name	Enter your paternal grandmother's name
Paternal Grandmother's Date of Birth	Enter her date of birth
Paternal Grandmother's Date of Death (if applicable)	Enter the date of death
Maternal Grandfather's Name	Enter your maternal grandfather's name

Maternal Grandfather's Date of Birth	Enter the date of birth
Maternal Grandfather's Date of Death (if applicable)	Enter the date of death
Maternal Grandmother's Name	Enter your maternal grandmother's name
Maternal Grandmother's Date of Birth	Enter the date of birth
Maternal Grandmother's Date of Death (if applicable)	Enter the date of death
Documents Location	Physical or digital location of grandparents' birth/marriage certificates
Earlier Ancestors (Great-Grandparents and Beyond)	
Great-Grandfather's Name	Record name of your great-grandfather (if known)
Great-Grandmother's Name	Enter the name of your great-grandmother (if known)
Historical Events/Details	Include any important historical events, stories, or details about this generation
Family Origin	Enter details about the family's country or region of origin
Documents Location	Physical or digital location of historical records, photos, or documents

Tip 1: Record family lineage details, such as birth dates, marriage dates, and significant milestones.

Tip 2: Encourage family members to contribute to the family tree for a more comprehensive record.

Tip 3: Digitize historical documents or photos for preservation.

Chapter 21: Safeguarding Important Documents in a Secure Vault (Digital and Physical)

"PROPERLY STORING IMPORTANT DOCUMENTS TODAY MEANS YOUR FAMILY CAN ACCESS THEM WITHOUT UNNECESSARY DELAYS OR STRESS WHEN THEY NEED THEM MOST."

Overview: Safeguarding critical documents, such as passports, birth certificates, property deeds, wills, and insurance policies, in a secure and easily accessible location ensures that your family can quickly access them when needed. During difficult times, especially following the death of a loved one, it can be overwhelming for family members to search for essential paperwork scattered across various locations. Keeping these documents in one organized and secure place, such as a digital vault or physical safe, prevents delays in settling legal matters, accessing accounts, or carrying out last wishes.

In addition to storing these documents digitally, it is also essential to maintain a physical copy of this book, along with other important information. The book provides a comprehensive guide to your family's financial and personal matters, making it a valuable resource when digital access is not possible. Keeping this book in a dedicated physical safe or a secure locker ensures that all the critical information remains readily available when needed most.

It's crucial to maintain an updated record of where these documents are stored and to inform trusted family members of how to access them. By ensuring that both digital and physical copies of these important documents and records are organized, you can provide your family with peace of mind, enabling them to navigate challenging situations smoothly and without added stress.

Real-Life Example:

1. When Geeta's mother passed away, her family was left scrambling to find important documents such as her will, insurance papers, and property deeds. These documents were scattered throughout the house in different drawers and files. It took weeks to gather everything, delaying tasks like transferring property ownership, claiming insurance benefits, and closing

bank accounts. The lack of organization added unnecessary stress during an already difficult time. If Geeta's mother had stored all of these documents in a secure vault and provided her family with access instructions, the process would have been much smoother and less emotionally taxing.

2. After billionaire **Howard Hughes** passed away in 1976, there was immense confusion over his estate due to a lack of accessible, well-organized documents. Various wills and claims surfaced, and it took several years of legal battles to settle his estate. Had Hughes stored his documents securely and made his intentions clear, the disputes and delays could have been avoided, and the process of distributing his assets would have been far more efficient and transparent.

Actionable Steps:

1. Store all **personal identification, financial, real estate, insurance, wills,** and **legal documents** in a secure location, ensuring that both physical and digital copies are accessible.
2. Maintain a clear record of **business** and **educational documents**, noting their physical or digital locations for easy access.
3. Keep track of **digital assets and passwords** securely, either through a password manager or a well-protected digital vault.
4. Regularly update **warranties and receipts** for high-value purchases, ensuring that documents are available if claims need to be made.

This **Document Vault Tracker** allows you to organize and securely store critical documents for yourself and your family. Using **FamilyCEO.in**, you can ensure that all essential paperwork is easy to locate and access, giving your family peace of mind in case of emergencies or when needed.

Tip 1: Store original copies of vital documents, like passports and birth certificates, in a secure, fireproof location.

Tip 2: Keep digital backups of all important documents in cloud storage.

Tip 3: Periodically review the inventory to ensure all documents are accounted for.

"After my husband's sudden death, I didn't know where our emergency funds were or how to access them. Something like Family CEO, where all emergency resources are tracked and stored, would have made all the difference in ensuring financial stability for our family right away."

- Kalpana Bandopadhyay, Kolkata

Chapter 22: Ensuring Access to Emergency Funds During Crisis

"ENSURING EASY ACCESS TO EMERGENCY FUNDS TODAY MEANS YOUR FAMILY CAN NAVIGATE TOUGH TIMES WITHOUT FINANCIAL STRESS."

Overview: Immediate access to emergency funds is essential for your family to cover urgent expenses, such as medical bills, funeral costs, or day-to-day living expenses, after your passing. In times of loss, financial stress can add to the emotional burden, and having an emergency fund in place helps ensure that your family's basic needs are met without unnecessary worry. This emergency fund can include a combination of easily accessible savings, insurance payouts, and short-term investments specifically designated for emergency use.

By defining these funds clearly, your family can focus on what truly matters—supporting one another—rather than worrying about how to cover unexpected costs. Whether it's immediate hospital bills, expenses for funeral arrangements, or simply keeping up with the household bills, a well-planned emergency fund acts as a financial safety net during an already difficult time.

Proper documentation of how and where to access these funds is also critical. This includes listing bank accounts, insurance policies, and any short-term investments that can be easily liquidated if needed. Providing key contacts for insurance companies, banks, and financial institutions will allow your loved ones to quickly locate and access the funds without delays or complications. Additionally, it's important to include any necessary account numbers, policy details, and instructions for accessing the funds, so there is no confusion about what to do.

Real-Life Example:

1. In 2016, **David Bowie**, the iconic musician, passed away after battling cancer. Due to Bowie's careful estate planning, his family had immediate access to emergency funds, including insurance payouts and investments, ensuring that they were able to cover funeral costs and other immediate expenses without financial strain. His well-documented estate included details about how to access these funds, providing his family with financial stability during an emotionally challenging time. Bowie's preparation

highlights the importance of organizing emergency funds and ensuring that they are easily accessible when needed most.

2. When actor **Heath Ledger** passed away in 2008, he had not updated his will to reflect the birth of his daughter, and as a result, accessing his assets became complex. While his family eventually managed to secure her financial future, there were significant delays in accessing funds to cover immediate expenses due to the lack of an updated estate plan. If Ledger had maintained a more structured plan with immediate access to emergency funds, the financial burden on his family during that period would have been reduced. This example underscores the importance of organizing emergency funds and updating estate plans to reflect life changes.

Actionable Steps:
- Document all **emergency cash reserves**, including access information and authorized persons.
- Track **bank accounts** and **short-term investments** that can be easily accessed during an emergency, ensuring clear access instructions are in place.
- Include **insurance payouts**, detailing the process to claim them, along with contact information for the insurance provider.
- Record any **loans or advances** given, tracking repayment schedules and access to these funds if needed.
- Clearly specify who is **authorized** to access these funds in case of emergency, providing detailed instructions for family members.

Emergency Funds Tracker Template

Category	Details (Fill it with a blue or black pen)
Cash Reserves	
Source of Funds	(Savings Account, Emergency Cash Stash, etc.)
Account Number (if applicable)	Enter the bank account number for emergency savings
Bank Name/Institution	Enter the name of the bank or financial institution

Current Balance	Enter the current balance of emergency cash reserves
Access Method	(ATM, Bank Transfer, Cash at Home, etc.)
Location of Cash (if applicable)	Enter physical location if cash is stored at home
Beneficiary/Authorized Person	Enter the name of the person authorized to access these funds
Documents Location	Physical or digital location of cash reserve records
Bank Accounts	
Account Type	(Savings, Checking, Joint, etc.)
Bank Name	Enter the name of the bank
Account Number	Enter the account number
Current Balance	Enter the current balance
Nominee/Authorized Person	Enter the name of the nominee or authorized person
Access Information	Enter login credentials or method of access
Documents Location	Physical or digital location of bank statements or records
Insurance Payouts	
Insurance Type	(Life, Health, Property, etc.)
Insurance Provider Name	Enter the name of the insurance company
Policy Number	Enter the insurance policy number
Beneficiary	Enter the name of the beneficiary for the insurance payout
Estimated Payout Amount	Enter the estimated payout amount in case of claim
Claim Process Instructions	Enter step-by-step instructions on how to claim the payout
Insurance Documents Location	Physical or digital location of insurance policy documents
Short-Term Investments	
Investment Type	(Mutual Fund, Fixed Deposit, Bonds, etc.)
Financial Institution Name	Enter the name of the institution handling the investment
Account/Policy Number	Enter the account or policy number

Current Value	Enter the current value of the investment
Maturity Date (if applicable)	Enter the maturity date, if applicable
Nominee/Authorized Person	Enter the name of the nominee or authorized person
Access Information	Provide access information and instructions
Documents Location	Physical or digital location of investment records
Loans and Advances (Given)	
Loan Recipient	Enter the name of the person or institution to whom the loan was given
Loan Amount	Enter the total loan amount
Outstanding Balance	Enter the current outstanding balance, if applicable
Repayment Terms	Specify the repayment schedule and terms
Next Payment Due Date	Enter the date of the next repayment
Documents Location	Physical or digital location of loan agreements or records
Access to Funds	
Authorized Person Name	Enter the name of the person authorized to access funds in case of emergency
Contact Information	Enter their phone number and email address
Power of Attorney (if applicable)	Enter the details of any power of attorney, if required
Location of Authorization Documents	Physical or digital location of power of attorney or authorization documents
Instructions for Immediate Use	
Instructions for Family	Provide clear instructions on how to access emergency funds immediately after a death or incapacitation
Critical Accounts to Access	List critical accounts to be accessed first (savings, insurance, pension, etc.)
Documents Location	Physical or digital location of critical instructions and documents

Tip 1: Maintain a list of emergency cash reserves, savings accounts, and insurance payouts.

Tip 2: Provide instructions on how to access these funds in case of emergency.

Tip 3: Keep contact information for banks and insurance providers handy.

As a parent of a child with special needs, I constantly worry about how his care will be handled if something happens to us. If we had a resource like Family CEO to organize our trust and legal documents, I'd feel much more at ease knowing his future is secure."

- Rajesh Lokhande, Kanpur

Chapter 23: Managing trusts for Special Needs Care and elderly parents

Overview:

Setting up a dedicated tracker for ***children with special needs*** is one of the most crucial steps a parent can take to ensure their child's well-being in all situations, especially in the event of an unfortunate accident or sudden loss. As a deeply emotional person, it's hard to imagine what your child could go through— facing the hardships of life without you or both parents. The fear of leaving them unprepared, vulnerable, and without a guiding hand can be overwhelming. That's why it's essential to think everything through carefully and make provisions for every possible need they may have.

This tracker is designed to comprehensively cover all aspects of your child's care—medical, financial, educational, and emotional—ensuring that their unique needs are documented in detail and accessible to caregivers or guardians. It provides clear guidance on medical care, including specific treatments, medications, healthcare providers, and emergency contacts. It also details long-term financial plans, such as savings, insurance policies, and investments that are in place for their future.

Educational needs are also carefully documented, whether it's information about special schools, individualized learning plans, or extracurricular activities that support their development. Moreover, emotional support is not forgotten—this tracker includes notes on what comforts your child, their preferences, routines, and anything that helps them feel secure and loved.

By organizing everything—from medical care to emotional comfort—this tracker ensures that even if the unthinkable happens, your child will not be left facing uncertainty or lack of care. It helps ensure that those stepping into a caregiving role have the information they need to provide the best possible support, minimizing confusion or delays. This dedicated tracker is your way of ensuring that, no matter what, your child will be provided for and protected, allowing them to navigate life's challenges without feeling abandoned or overwhelmed.

Tracker for elderly parents:

This book also provides a dedicated tracker for elderly parents, ensuring their care is thoughtfully managed in every aspect. Just like a child with special needs, elderly parents are equally vulnerable in the absence of their caregiver. They may depend on you for their medical, financial, and emotional support, and ensuring their needs are met is just as crucial.

This tracker allows you to document all essential aspects of your elderly parents' care—medical history, medications, healthcare providers, financial details, and specific preferences. It provides detailed guidance for caregivers, ensuring that your parents receive consistent, uninterrupted care even in your absence.

Information such as scheduled medical appointments, dietary preferences, emergency contacts, and financial arrangements for their well-being are all included. By having everything documented clearly, those taking over the caregiving responsibilities can understand and address your parents' needs effectively. This reduces their vulnerability and ensures they continue to receive the love, attention, and care they deserve, even during challenging times.

Real-Life Example:

1. In the United States, **Heather McLaughlin** faced the sudden loss of her husband, Logan, who had set up a special needs trust for their son with autism. Logan had made thorough plans to ensure their son's financial and medical care would continue in the event of his death. However, due to the complexity of the trust's instructions and the lack of clear documentation for the caregivers, Heather encountered delays in accessing the trust's funds and coordinating care. This situation caused significant financial strain and emotional stress, which could have been avoided if Logan had documented the necessary contact details, instructions, and access protocols in a clear and organized manner.

2. In 2017, the **Boyes family** in the UK lost their son's primary caregiver—his father—unexpectedly. The son had Down syndrome, and while the father had arranged for a special needs trust, the family had no information on how to contact the trustee or access the funds quickly. Additionally, there were no detailed instructions regarding the child's day-to-day care needs, including his medical treatments and educational requirements. This resulted in months of confusion and financial instability for the family. With better documentation of care plans and financial arrangements, the family could have avoided many of these challenges.

3. In Canada, **Marjorie and Wesley Spears** faced a similar challenge when Wesley, who was the primary caregiver for their daughter with cerebral palsy, passed away. Wesley had set up a trust to ensure her future care but hadn't provided a detailed plan for her ongoing medical treatments, therapies, or who would take over her care. As a result, it took the family several months to sort out the legal and financial paperwork, delaying access to vital funds and services. Had Wesley documented this information more thoroughly, the transition of care would have been far less complicated and stressful.

Actionable Steps

- Fill in the child's medical history, including diagnoses, treatment plans, and a list of medications, ensuring that any caregivers or emergency personnel have access to this information.

- Document the primary and backup caregivers, including contact details and any special instructions regarding daily care routines, dietary needs, and communication methods.

- Ensure financial planning is in place by detailing any trusts, government benefits, or savings plans set up for the child's long-term care and education, along with clear instructions for accessing these funds.

- Include educational information, such as current special education programs, IEPs (Individualized Education Plans), and future educational goals, ensuring continuity of education.

- Store legal documents, such as guardianship papers, power of attorney, and trust documents, in an easily accessible and secure location for family members and legal advisors.

- Provide emergency contact details, including doctors, therapists, and counselors who are familiar with the child's specific needs, so they can be reached quickly in case of an emergency.

- Outline long-term care arrangements and financial planning to ensure the child's future medical, housing, and caregiving needs are met, with clear instructions for trustees or caregivers.

- Regularly update the tracker as the child's medical needs, caregivers, or financial situation changes to ensure the most accurate and up-to-date information is available.

This **Special Needs Care Tracker** helps ensure that all critical information related to your child's medical, financial, educational, and legal needs is documented in an organized way. By using the FamilyCEO.in platform to upload and store this information, you provide caregivers and trustees with easy access to vital resources, ensuring your child's well-being and care in your absence.

Tip 1: Document the special care requirements, including specific medical treatments, medications, and daily routines.

Tip 2: Provide a list of legal guardians or caregivers responsible for managing the care.

Tip 3: Update the tracker periodically to reflect any changes in care needs or financial arrangements

23A: Special Needs Care Tracker

Category	Details (Fill it with a blue or black pen)
Medical Information and Ongoing Care	
Current Diagnoses and Treatment Plans	List the child's medical conditions, treatment plans, and schedules.
Doctors and Specialists	Contact details of primary doctors, specialists, and health care providers.
Medications and Treatment Schedules	List of medications, doses, and timing, along with ongoing treatments.
Insurance Information	Details of health insurance policies and coverage for special needs care.
Emergency Procedures	Specific steps to take in case of a medical emergency related to their health conditions.
Financial Planning	
Pension and Trust Accounts	Details of trusts, long-term savings, and instructions on how to access them.
Bank Account Information	Bank account details, including access information and authorized signatories.
Trusts and Financial Guardianship	Information about trusts set up for the child, including trustee contact information.
Caregivers and Guardians	
Primary Caregiver Information	Contact details of the designated caregiver for their support.
Backup Caregivers	Contact details of secondary or emergency caregivers.
Special Instructions for Care	Specific instructions or routines, including needs and preferences the child may require.
Daily Routine and Preferences	
Dietary Requirements	Information on dietary preferences, restrictions, and meal schedules.

Daily Schedule and Activities	Details of daily routines, favourite activities, and items that bring comfort.
Personal Comfort Preferences	Notes on anything that brings emotional comfort, like favorite music, books, or pictures.
Legal Documentation	
Wills and Estate Planning	Documents outlining inheritance, estate plans, and legal wishes for the child's care.
Power of Attorney	Power of attorney details for medical and financial decisions.
Guardianship and Legal Protections	Information on legal guardianship or any court orders regarding their care.
Long-Term Care Planning	
Lifetime Financial Planning	Long-term financial planning for medical care, housing, and daily living expenses.
Living Arrangements	Plans for current and future housing arrangements, including information on assisted living if needed.
Emotional and Psychological Support	
Counseling and Therapy Services	Contact information for counselors, therapists, or emotional support resources.
Support Networks	List of support groups, community networks, or organizations that can provide assistance for the child during difficult times.

Personal Notes

23B: Elderly Parents' Care Tracker

Category	Details (Fill it with a blue or black pen)
Medical Information and Ongoing Care	
Current Diagnoses and Treatment Plans	
Doctors and Specialists	
Medications and Treatment Schedules	
Insurance Information	
Emergency Procedures	
Financial Planning	
Pension and Retirement Accounts	
Bank Account Information	
Trusts and Financial Guardianship	
Caregivers and Guardians	
Primary Caregiver Information	
Backup Caregivers	
Special Instructions for Care	
Daily Routine and Preferences	
Dietary Requirements	
Daily Schedule and Activities	

Personal Comfort Preferences	Notes on anything that brings emotional comfort, like religious items, favorite books or music.
Legal Documentation	
Wills and Estate Planning	Documents outlining inheritance, estate plans, and final wishes.
Power of Attorney	Power of attorney details for medical and financial decisions.
Guardianship and Legal Protections	Information on legal guardianship, or any court orders regarding their care.
Long-Term Care Planning	
Lifetime Financial Planning	Long-term financial planning for medical care, housing, and daily living expenses.
Living Arrangements	Plans for current and future housing arrangements, including information on assisted living or nursing facilities if needed.
Emotional and Psychological Support	
Counseling and Therapy Services	Contact information for counselors, therapists, or emotional support resources.
Support Networks	List of support groups, community networks, or organizations that can provide assistance to family, pets used in difficult times.

Personal Notes

Chapter 24: Closing Accounts and Settling Affairs After Death

"PROPERLY DOCUMENTING HOW TO CLOSE ACCOUNTS AND SETTLE AFFAIRS ENSURES THAT YOUR LOVED ONES CAN FOCUS ON HEALING, RATHER THAN NAVIGATING COMPLEX FINANCIAL TASKS."

Overview: Documenting the process for closing bank accounts, paying off loans, and canceling subscriptions is an essential step to ensure that your financial affairs are settled smoothly and efficiently after your passing. During an already emotionally difficult time, dealing with financial matters can become overwhelming for your family, especially if they are left without clear guidance. Without explicit instructions, your family may struggle to figure out which accounts and loans need to be closed, potentially resulting in overdue bills, continued payments for unused services, and financial stress that could easily have been avoided.

Organizing this information in a dedicated tracker, which includes account details, loan payoff instructions, and contact information for service providers, provides your loved ones with a clear roadmap. This tracker should detail every bank account that needs to be closed, any loans that must be settled, and instructions on how to handle each. It should also include information on recurring subscriptions—such as utilities, digital services, or memberships—that will need to be canceled.

By providing a structured plan, you spare your loved ones from having to piece together fragmented information while they are grieving. They will know exactly whom to contact, what paperwork is required, and what steps to take to close each account, pay off debts, and prevent unnecessary expenses. This proactive approach ensures that financial obligations are met, preventing confusion, legal complications, or penalties associated with late payments or unclosed accounts. Ultimately, it is a way to protect your family from added burdens and to give them peace of mind, knowing that all affairs are properly managed and settled.

Real-Life Example:
1. After Ashok passed away, his family faced difficulties managing his various credit card accounts, loans, and subscriptions. They were unsure which

accounts were active and which ones had been paid off. As a result, bills continued to pile up, and they didn't know which ones needed to be canceled. It took months to sort out his financial obligations, causing unnecessary stress and financial strain. Had Ashok documented his accounts and provided clear instructions for closing them, his family could have handled the process much more smoothly and avoided ongoing payments.

2. When celebrity chef **Anthony Bourdain** passed away in 2018, his estate was left well-organized, which made it easier for his family and legal team to settle his affairs. Bourdain had clear documentation of his financial accounts, loans, and assets, which streamlined the process of closing accounts and paying off debts. His attention to detail and preparation ensured that his loved ones were spared from financial confusion and additional stress during their time of grief. This case illustrates the importance of maintaining up-to-date records of financial accounts and closing instructions for an orderly and efficient settlement of affairs.

Actionable Steps:

- Document the closure process for **bank accounts, credit cards, loans, investments, and insurance policies**. Ensure that family members or authorized persons have clear instructions on the necessary steps.
- List required **documents** for closing accounts (death certificate, proof of identity, etc.), and keep these documents in a secure, easily accessible location.
- Include contact information for **service providers** (financial institutions, digital services, and utilities) to simplify the closure process for family members.
- Ensure that an **authorized person** is designated to handle all closures and account settlements, providing Power of Attorney if necessary.

Tip 1: Document account closure procedures for all bank accounts, credit cards, and subscriptions.
Tip 2: Keep a checklist of necessary steps for settling debts, such as paying outstanding bills.
Tip 3: Update records periodically to ensure all accounts are listed.

Closing Accounts in Case of Death Tracker Template

Category	Details (Fill it with a blue or black pen)
Bank Accounts	
Bank Name	Enter the name of the bank
Account Number	Enter the account number
Type of Account	(Savings, Checking, Joint, etc.)
Nominee Name	Enter the name of the nominee
Required Documents	(Death certificate, proof of identity, nomination form, etc.)
Closure Process	Enter step-by-step instructions on closing the account
Bank Contact Information	Bank branch contact number and email
Closure Timeline	Estimated time to process account closure
Documents Location	Physical or digital location
Credit Cards	
Issuing Bank/Card Provider	Enter the name of the credit card issuer
Credit Card Number	Enter the last four digits of the credit card number
Outstanding Balance	Enter the current outstanding balance, if any
Nominee/Authorized Person	Enter the name of the nominee or authorized person
Required Documents	(Death certificate, proof of identity, etc.)
Closure Process	Instructions on closing the credit card, including contact information
Documents Location	Physical or digital location of credit card documents
Loans and Mortgages	
Loan Provider Name	Enter the name of the loan provider (bank, financial institution)
Loan Account Number	Enter the loan account number
Loan Type	(Home Loan, Car Loan, Personal Loan, etc.)
Outstanding Balance	Enter the current outstanding loan amount

Nominee/Authorized Person	Enter the name of the person responsible for handling the item
Required Documents	(Death certificate, loan agreement, etc.)
Closure Process	Provide instructions on settling or closing the loan account
Documents Location	Physical or digital location of loan documents
Investment Accounts	
Investment Provider Name	Enter the name of the investment provider (mutual funds, stocks, etc.)
Account Number/Policy Number	Enter the account or policy number
Current Value	Enter the current value of the investment
Nominee Name	Enter the name of the nominee
Required Documents	(Death certificate, nominee form, proof of identity)
Closure Process	Step-by-step instructions on how to close or transfer the investment
Provider Contact Information	Enter the contact details of the investment provider
Documents Location	Physical or digital location of investment records
Insurance Policies	
Insurance Provider Name	Enter the name of the insurance company
Policy Number	Enter the insurance policy number
Type of Insurance	(Life, health, home, etc.)
Nominee Name	Enter the name of the nominee
Required Documents	(Death certificate, proof of identity, nominee form)
Claim/Closure Process	Instructions on filing a claim or closing the policy
Provider Contact Information	Enter the contact details of the insurance company
Documents Location	Physical or digital location of insurance policies

Digital Accounts	
Account Type	(Email, Social media, Cloud Storage, etc.)
Service Provider	Enter the name of the service provider.
Username/Email	Enter the username or email linked.
Closure Process	Instructions for closing the digital account, including any specific protocols.
Required Documents	(Death certificate, account information, proof of identity)
Provider Contact Information	Enter the contact details of the service provider.
Documents Location	Physical or digital location of account details and passwords.
Utility Accounts	
Utility Type	(Electricity, Water, Gas, Internet, etc.)
Account Number	Enter the utility account number.
Provider Name	Enter the name of the service provider.
Closure Process	Instructions for closing the utility account.
Required Documents	(Death certificate, proof of residence, etc.)
Provider Contact Information	Enter the contact details of the utility provider.
Documents Location	Physical or digital location of utility bills/records.
Subscriptions & Memberships	
Subscription Type	(Streaming Services, Gym Memberships, Magazine Subscriptions, etc.)
Provider Name	Enter the name of the subscription or service provider.
Account Number/Subscription ID	Enter the subscription account number or ID.
Closure Process	Provide instructions on how to cancel the subscription.
Required Documents	(Death certificate, proof of identity, etc.)
Provider Contact Information	Enter the contact details of the subscription provider.
Documents Location	Physical or digital location of subscription agreement.

Contact for Handling Accounts	
Authorized Person Name	Enter the name of the person authorized to handle account closures
Relationship to Deceased	Enter the relationship to the deceased
Contact Information	Enter the phone number and email of the authorized person
Power of Attorney (if applicable)	Enter any Power of Attorney details
Documents Location	Physical or digital location of Power of Attorney documents

Personal Notes

MANAGING EMERGENCY FUNDS

Establishing and managing emergency funds is crucial for protecting your family during unforeseen circumstances. Here are the best practices to ensure that your emergency funds are effective and readily available:

1. Determine the Right Amount

3-6 Months of Living Expenses: Generally, an emergency fund should cover 3 to 6 months of essential living expenses, such as rent/mortgage, utilities, food, and healthcare. For added security, you could consider saving up to a year's worth of expenses.

Evaluate Specific Needs: If your family has special needs, such as ongoing medical care or dependents, consider increasing the size of your emergency fund to cover these costs comfortably.

2. Keep Funds Accessible

Liquid Accounts: Store your emergency funds in accounts that offer easy and quick access, such as a high-yield savings account or money market account. Avoid tying up emergency funds in investments that are hard to liquidate, like real estate or long-term bonds.

Avoid Withdrawal Penalties: Ensure the account you use for emergency funds doesn't carry penalties for withdrawals, making it easy to access whenever needed.

3. Separate from Regular Savings

Dedicated Account: Keep your emergency funds in a separate account from your regular savings to prevent mixing and accidentally spending the money. This separation helps maintain the fund's purpose solely for emergencies.

4. Automate Contributions

Automatic Transfers: Set up automatic transfers from your checking account to your emergency fund to make saving consistent and hassle-free. This way, you'll build your emergency fund without having to think about it actively.

Set Monthly Targets: Define monthly contribution goals to ensure you steadily build your emergency fund over time.

5. Avoid Investing Emergency Funds

Focus on Security, Not Growth: Emergency funds should be kept in low-risk, stable accounts. Avoid investing them in the stock market or other volatile options where their value could decline, making them inaccessible in a crisis.

Low Risk, Low Return: The main objective is accessibility and stability, not maximizing returns. Focus on financial instruments that offer easy access with minimal risk.

6. Ensure Emergency Fund Accessibility for Your Family

Document Access Instructions: Clearly document how to access the emergency funds, including account numbers, bank details, and authorized users. Keep these instructions in a secure location and share them with trusted family members.

Joint Account or POD (Payable on Death): Consider setting up a joint account with your spouse or adding a trusted person as a beneficiary or POD on the account. This ensures quick access in case you are not around.

7. Regularly Review and Update Fund Size

Annual Reassessment: Review your emergency fund at least once a year to ensure that it matches your current living expenses, especially if there have been major changes like a new family member, a change in income, or increased expenses.

Adjust for Inflation: Make sure your emergency fund keeps pace with inflation, increasing the amount periodically to maintain your purchasing power.

8. Diversify Emergency Fund Locations

Multiple Accounts for Safety: To minimize risk, consider keeping emergency funds in two different locations (e.g., two separate banks or accounts). This provides a backup if one bank is temporarily inaccessible.

Cash at Hand: Keep a small amount of cash in a secure place at home for immediate needs in situations where electronic banking might not be possible.

9. Avoid Using Funds for Non-Emergencies

Reserve Only for True Emergencies: Avoid dipping into your emergency fund for non-urgent expenses like vacations, home improvements, or discretionary spending. It should only be used for unexpected events like medical emergencies, job loss, or major home repairs.

Define Emergency Scenarios: Clearly define what qualifies as an emergency (e.g., sudden medical expenses, urgent home repairs) to avoid unnecessary withdrawals.

10. Document a Backup Plan

Create an Emergency Fund Tracker: Maintain a tracker that lists account details, access information, and specific instructions for family members. This should be included with other important documents so that loved ones can access funds smoothly if necessary.

Communicate with Family Members: Inform at least two trusted individuals where the emergency fund is located and how they can access it in case they need to act on your behalf.

11. Set Up Contingency Funding Options

Line of Credit: Consider having a low-interest line of credit as an additional layer of security if your emergency fund needs to be supplemented.

Insurance Policies: Ensure you have health, home, and life insurance policies to reduce potential out-of-pocket expenses that would otherwise need to come from your emergency fund.

PHYSICAL DOCUMENT BACKUPS

Securing physical document backups is an important step to ensure that your family can easily access critical information in times of need. Here are some key methods to effectively safeguard physical documents:

1. Fireproof and Waterproof Safe

Invest in a Fireproof and Waterproof Safe: A high-quality safe provides protection against natural disasters, such as fires and floods, ensuring that your critical documents remain intact. Make sure it is locked securely and installed in a discreet location within your home.

Keep Essential Documents Inside: Store items like wills, insurance policies, property deeds, and financial records in the safe.

2. Bank Safety Deposit Box

Use a Bank Safety Deposit Box: A safety deposit box at your bank provides an extra layer of security. Store original copies of documents, such as deeds, investment papers, or irreplaceable valuables, in the box.

Keep a Copy at Home: Keep a physical copy of important documents at home for quick reference, in case the originals are stored in the bank.

3. Multiple Copies

Create Multiple Copies: Make multiple copies of critical documents—one for the bank safety deposit box, one in the safe at home, and possibly another for a trusted relative or legal advisor.

Mark Copies Clearly: Label each copy and indicate where the originals are stored to prevent confusion.

4. Laminate Frequently Used Documents

Lamination for Durability: Documents like birth certificates, identity cards, and passports that might be handled frequently can be laminated to avoid wear and tear. This step will help to preserve their condition.

5. Organize in a Filing System

Use an Organized Filing System: Store copies in an organized filing system with clearly labeled folders. Include sections such as "Legal Documents," "Financial Records," "Insurance Policies," etc.

Color-Coded Folders: Consider color-coded folders for easy identification, and use dividers to group documents by type.

6. Secure Location

Keep Backups in Different Locations: Don't store all copies in the same location. Spread them across a home safe, a bank safety deposit box, and another trusted location to minimize risk from theft or damage.

Choose a Trusted Person: If you opt to store copies with a family member or friend, choose someone reliable who understands the importance of these documents and the need for confidentiality.

7. Document Inventory List

Maintain an Inventory List: Create an inventory list of all the important documents you have, including where they are stored. This list should be kept in your safe and with a trusted person so your family can quickly find out what's available and where it is located.

8. Emergency Folder

Prepare an Emergency "Grab-and-Go" Folder: For times when you need to leave home quickly (such as in an emergency), have an easily accessible folder with the most critical documents (such as identification, insurance papers, and medical records).

9. Use Document Holders

Store in Waterproof Document Holders: Even within the safe, place important documents in waterproof holders to add an extra layer of protection, especially against moisture or minor leaks.

10. Communicate Locations to Trusted Persons

Inform Family Members or Trusted Friends: Make sure that at least two trusted family members or close friends know where to find the documents and have access to the safe or bank deposit box if necessary. Share a detailed list and clear instructions on how to retrieve the documents.

The **Digital Vault** tab on **www.familyceo.in** is designed to provide your family with secure access to all critical documents and information in one place. Managing this digital vault effectively will ensure that important details are readily available when needed, while maintaining the highest level of security. Here are some best practices for managing the digital vault on **www.FamilyCEO.in**:

1. Store Copies of Critical Documents

Upload Scanned Copies: Use the Digital Vault to upload scanned copies of essential documents, such as passports, birth certificates, property deeds, wills, insurance policies, and financial statements. Ensure that each document is clearly labeled and organized by type.

Keep Documents Updated: Regularly update copies to reflect the most recent versions, especially when there are changes in financial information, healthcare plans, or legal arrangements.

2. Organize Information into Categories

Use Categories and Tags: Within the Digital Vault tab, organize documents into distinct categories such as "Financial," "Medical," "Legal," "Insurance," and "Personal." This structure will help your family quickly locate the information they need during critical moments.

Important Contacts: Create a section for important contacts, including lawyers, doctors, financial advisors, and emergency contacts, with their phone numbers and email addresses readily accessible.

3. Enable Secure Access for Trusted People

Assign Access to Trusted Family Members: You can assign specific permissions for trusted family members, such as read-only or full access, depending on their role. For example, your spouse may have full access, while another trusted relative may have read-only access.

Backup Trustee: Designate a backup trustee—such as a close relative or legal advisor—who can access the Digital Vault if you are unable to do so.

4. Use Strong, Unique Passwords

Create Strong Credentials: Set a strong, unique password for accessing www.FamilyCEO.in, combining letters, numbers, and special characters. Avoid using easily guessed information like birthdays.

Password Manager: Use a password manager to store the credentials for www.FamilyCEO.in, ensuring they are secure and easily accessible when needed.

5. Enable Two-Factor Authentication (2FA)

Add Extra Security: Enable two-factor authentication (2FA) on your www.FamilyCEO.in account to provide an additional layer of security. This will ensure that unauthorized access to your Digital Vault is prevented, even if the password is compromised.

6. Document Access Instructions for Loved Ones

Clear Instructions: Document the process for accessing the Digital Vault and share it with trusted family members. Include details such as the website link, username, and the process to complete the two-factor authentication.

Backup Credentials: Store a physical copy of these access details in a fireproof and waterproof safe at home or in a bank safety deposit box.

7. Regularly Review and Update Content

Periodic Reviews: Set a reminder to review and update the contents of your Digital Vault at least once or twice a year. Make sure that all the documents are current and that any outdated versions are removed.

Log Changes: Keep a record of the changes made within the Digital Vault so that family members can track what has been updated.

8. Store a Backup of Digital Vault Data

External Backup: Regularly download an encrypted backup of the documents stored in the Digital Vault. Store this backup on an encrypted USB drive, which can be kept in a secure location such as a home safe or bank deposit box.

Update Backups: Update the backup whenever you make significant changes to the Digital Vault, ensuring that it always reflects the latest information.

9. Test Access with Trusted Individuals

Practice Accessing the Vault: Schedule a "practice run" with a trusted family member to ensure they know how to access the Digital Vault on www.FamilyCEO.in. This will help identify any issues beforehand and provide confidence during an actual emergency. Also, Review Access Permissions Regularly.

10. Use Secure Devices and Avoid Public Networks

Secure Access Points: Only access the Digital Vault from secure, private devices that have updated antivirus software. Avoid using public networks or shared devices, as they can be vulnerable to cyber-attacks.

Malware Protection: Ensure that your devices are protected from malware and run periodic scans to prevent unauthorized access.

FAMILY VALUES TRACKER

Benefits of Including a Family Values Tracker

1. **Guiding Principles for Future Generations**: Clearly documenting your family values helps provide guidance to your children and grandchildren on how they should approach life, relationships, and challenges.

2. **Strengthen Family Bonds**: Having a written record of shared values creates a sense of unity and collective identity, helping strengthen family bonds, especially when members are apart.

3. **Personal Accountability**: This tracker also acts as a reminder for everyone to stay accountable to their values. Family members can refer to it during difficult situations to remind themselves of the core beliefs that should guide their actions.

4. **Legacy Beyond Wealth**: Material wealth can be passed on to future generations, but passing down values creates a richer legacy. Documenting values helps ensure that your family's core beliefs are not lost over time.

How to Use the Family Values Tracker

- **Regular Review**: Review the values as a family periodically, such as at family gatherings or during holidays. Discuss how each value has been upheld and share stories of how they impacted your lives.

- **Update as Needed**: Family values can evolve. Add new values or make adjustments as your family grows and changes.

- **Share Stories**: Record specific family stories and experiences that demonstrate the values in action. These examples will help future generations understand the importance of the values and make them feel more personal.

Core Value	Description	Traditions /Practices	Examples of How to Apply	Notes
Integrity	Always be honest and do what is right, even when no one is watching.	Family honesty discussions once a month	Lead by example in admitting mistakes and being transparent	Include examples of past family actions that show integrity.
Compassion	Show kindness and empathy to others, both inside and outside the family.	Volunteering at a local charity annually	Reach out to neighbors in need, offer help when someone is struggling	Note specific causes or charities the family supports.
Respect	Respect everyone, regardless of age, background, or opinion.	Respect elders and listen to their stories	Avoid interrupting when someone speaks, celebrate differences	Include stories that emphasize the value of respect.
Education	Value lifelong learning and strive to grow and improve.	Reading night every week, promoting curiosity	Encourage reading, share new things learned at the dinner table	Provide suggestions on educational activities for all ages.
Unity	Support and stand by each other in good times and bad.	Family dinners every Sunday	Encourage open communication, participate in each other's activities	Keep a family journal for shared memories and experiences.

Gratitude	Be thankful for what you have and express appreciation.	Daily gratitude reflection before bedtime	Write gratitude notes to each other, keep a family gratitude jar	Include tips on expressing gratitude in everyday life.
Resilience	Face challenges bravely, without giving up.	Celebrate overcoming challenges as a family	Remind each other of past difficult situations you overcame	Record family stories of resilience to inspire future generations.
Humility	Stay humble and avoid boasting. Recognize that every person has strengths and weaknesses.	Acknowledge others' achievements sincerely	Praise others, downplay one's own achievements, focus on group success	Note stories that demonstrate humility within the family.
Family First	Place family well-being above individual pursuits.	Spend holidays together, support family events	Set aside time for family activities, help family members when needed	Highlight the importance of prioritizing family over work or other commitments.

Overview:

The **Inheritance Distribution Tracker** is designed to provide a clear and organized record of how assets should be distributed among beneficiaries after your passing. Documenting this information helps to avoid confusion, prevent disputes, and ensure that your wishes are fulfilled smoothly. This tracker will also make it easier for the executor of your estate and your legal advisors to manage the process without unnecessary delays.

Instructions for Using the Tracker:

1. Asset Type and Description:

Clearly define each asset, such as real estate, bank accounts, investment accounts, personal items (like jewelry or vehicles), and business interests.

2. Beneficiary Details:

List each beneficiary's name and relationship to you (e.g., spouse, child, sibling).

Specify the percentage or value of each asset they will receive.

3. Location of Documents:

Indicate where the original documents related to each asset are kept, such as in a bank safety deposit box, home safe, or the digital vault on www.familyceo.in.

4. Special Instructions:

Provide any specific instructions for the distribution, such as timing or conditions for use (e.g., funds for education only).

Include details on any liabilities or expenses that need to be settled before distribution.

Benefits of an Inheritance Distribution Tracker:

1. Clarity for Your Loved Ones: By documenting how assets should be distributed, you remove any ambiguity that could lead to misunderstandings among your heirs.

2. Ease for Executors: This tracker provides detailed instructions for the executor of your estate, making their role easier and ensuring that your wishes are executed smoothly.

3. Avoid Legal Disputes: By being explicit about asset distribution, you help prevent potential legal disputes that could arise from ambiguity in your estate plan.

4. Ensuring Fairness: Each beneficiary knows exactly what they are entitled to, which helps maintain family harmony.

Regular Updates:

- Review and update the Inheritance Distribution Tracker whenever there are significant life events, such as the birth of a child, the acquisition or sale of property, or the death of a beneficiary. This will ensure that the information remains current and that your wishes are always clearly documented.

Sample Details to Include in the Tracker:

Asset Type	Description	Beneficiary	Percentage/Value	Location	Special Instructions
Property	12/A, MG Road, Mumbai	Madhura Sonar (Spouse)	100%	Registered Deed at SBI	Retain property for family residence
Bank Savings Account	SBI Account #123456789	Shaarav Sonar (Son)	50%	SBI Bank	Ensure funds are transferred after settling all liabilities
Investment Account	ICICI Securities #987654321	Shaleen Sonar (Daughter)	100%	ICICI Securities	Use funds for higher education
Jewelry	Gold Necklace	Shaleen Sonar (Daughter)	Full Item	Bank Safety Deposit Box	Hand over during her wedding
Vehicle	Honda City (Car)	Shreeyash Sonar (Brother)	Full Item	Parking Garage	Transfer title to Rajesh

Business Ownership	ABC Ventures (20% share)	Aarav & Shaleen Sonar	50% each	Business Registration Docs	Retain ownership, consult lawyer for succession planning

A few more sample Trackers (formatting reference only)

Sample Tracker for Real Estate Assets

Asset Type	Description	Beneficiary	Percentage/Value	Location	Special Instructions
Residential Property	12/A, MG Road, Mumbai	Madhura Sonar (Spouse)	100%	Registered Deed at SBI	Retain property for family residence.
Rental Property	45/B, Maple Ave, Pune	Shaarav Sonar (Son)	100%	HDFC Bank	Rental income to be used for Aarav's future expenses.

Sample Tracker for Bank Accounts and Financial Assets

Savings Account	SBI Account #123456789	Shaarav Sonar (Son)	50%	SBI Bank	Ensure funds are transferred after settling all liabilities.
Fixed Deposit	ICICI FD #987654321	Shaleen Sonar (Daughter)	100%	ICICI Bank	Maturity amount to be used for Aisha's higher education.
Mutual Fund	Axis Mutual Fund #789101112	Madhura Sonar (Spouse)	100%	Axis Mutual Fund	Redemption allowed at the discretion of the spouse.

Sample Tracker for Personal Items (Jewelry, Vehicles, Collectibles)

Jewelry	Gold Necklace	Shaleen Sonar (Daughter)	Full Item	Bank Safety Deposit Box	Hand over during her wedding.
Vehicle	Honda City (Car)	Shreeyash Sonar (Brother)	Full Item	Parking Garage	Transfer title to Rajesh after settling pending dues.

Painting	Traditional Indian Painting	Shaarav Sonar (Son)	Full Item	Home Living Room	To be kept in the family and not sold.

Sample Tracker for Business Ownership and Shares

Asset Type	Description	Beneficiary	Percentage/ Value	Location	Special Instructions
Business Ownership	ABC Ventures (20% share)	Shaarav & Shaleen Sonar	50% each	Business Registration Docs	Retain ownership and consult a lawyer for succession planning.
Partnership Interest	XYZ Enterprises (15% stake)	Madhura Sonar (Spouse)	100%	Business Contract File	Partner buyout clause must be reviewed by the spouse.

Sample Tracker for Insurance Policies and Retirement Accounts

Life Insurance	LIC Policy #987654321	Madhura Sonar (Spouse)	100%	Digital Vault at www.Family CEO.in	Use for children's education and spouse's financial security.
Retirement Fund	EPF Account #123456789	Shaarav Sonar (Son)	50%	EPF Office, Documents in Home Safe	Ensure no early withdrawals to avoid penalties.
Health Insurance	Family Floater Policy	Madhura Sonar (Spouse)	Full Benefit	Policy Documents in Home Safe	Premiums to be continued from savings account.

Sample Tracker for Digital Assets

Cryptocurrency	Bitcoin Wallet (5 BTC)	Shaarav Sonar (Son)	100%	Digital Vault at www.FamilyCEO.in	Use wallet key provided in the digital vault.
Domain Names	FamilyCEO.in	Shaleen Sonar (Daughter)	Full Ownership	Registrar Account Details	Renew annually, consider future sale or family use.

Sample Tracker for Heirlooms and Sentimental Items

Heirloom	Grandfather's Pocket Watch	Shaarav Sonar (Son)	Full Item	Home Safe	Pass down to the eldest male in each generation.
Family Album	Photo Album (1950-1980)	Shaleen Sonar (Daughter)	Full Item	Home Living Room	Preserve with care and add new family milestones.